£62·00

(2)

ROAD VEHICLE PERFORMANCE

Transportation Studies
A series edited by
NORMAN ASHFORD, Loughborough University of Technology
WILLIAM G. BELL, Florida State University

ISSN: 0278-3819

ROAD VEHICLE PERFORMANCE

Methods of Measurement and Calculation

G.G. Lucas

Loughborough University of Technology,
Loughborough, U.K.

GORDON AND BREACH
Switzerland · Australia · Belgium · France ·
Germany · Great Britain · India · Japan · Malaysia ·
Netherlands · Russia · Singapore · USA

First published 1986
Second printing 1994

ISBN 0-677-21400-6. ISSN 0278-3819. No part of this book may be reproduced or utilized in any form or by any means, electronic or mechanical, including photocopying and recording, or by any information storage or retrieval system, without permission in writing from the publisher. Printed in the United States of America.

Gordon and Breach Science Publishers
Y-Parc
Chemin de la Sallaz
1400 Yverdon, Switzerland

Library of Congress Cataloging-in-Publication Data

Lucas, G.G. (George Gordon)
    Road vehicle performance.
    (Transportation studies, ISSN 0278-3819; v. 7)
    Bibliography: p.
    1. Automobile engineering. I. Title. II. Series.
TL240.L76 1986   629.2   86-3120.
ISBN 0-677-21400-6

level 3

"Aos meus amigos brasileiros"

Contents

Preface

The incentive to write this book came from discussions with vehicle performance engineers in the automotive industry. The advent of computers has changed markedly the techniques and procedures used to calculate the performance of a vehicle. These later techniques have been researched at Loughborough. They are taught in the undergraduate course in "Automotive Engineering and Design" and the postgraduate short courses of "Road Vehicle Transmissions" and "Whole Vehicle Testing", but, apart from the course notes and technical papers, are not written down.

The vintage of these techniques is now such that they have been reasonably well tried and tested and are ready to appear in a text book.

I wish to acknowledge help from Hawker Siddeley Brush Electrical Machines Ltd., Loughborough, OECD in Paris, The Automobile Engineer, The Automotive Design Engineering, Goodyear International Tire Technical Centre of Luxembourg, Austin Rover Ltd., M.I.R.A. Leyland Vehicles, Sunstrand Ltd., BL Technology Ltd., and from my colleagues in the Department of Transport Technology, Loughborough University of Technology.

G.G. LUCAS

Introduction

The garnering of the material of this book started in 1961, at the birth of the "Automotive Enginering & Design" course at Loughborough. Its theories and practices have been honed on successive generations of students and tested by their application in industry.

The book is concerned with the accelerative performance: the maximum speed, gradeability and fuel consumption of road vehicles, particularly those of motor cars and trucks. Its contents may be used to estimate and measure the performance of other classes of vehicle, such as motor cycles, electric vehicles and railed vehicles, although these are not mentioned specifically within its pages. The scope of the book embraces the definition of terms, the calculation procedures and the test work associated with the term "performance" as defined above. The braking of road vehicles has been excluded because it is a subject in its own right and the topic of publications by colleagues.

In 1961, the tools of the performance engineer were the slide rule, charts and rule-of-thumb formulae. The digital computer was in its infancy. The now wide-spread use of this machine has allowed a more fundamental approach to performance calculations to be pursued, eliminating the need for tedious, repetitive and often iterative hand calculations. It is the computerized approach that is presented here. The performance models described have been written with the performance engineer and the designer in mind. The computer programs outlined are suitable for parametric studies; that is, a particular design or operating parameter may be successively altered in order that its effect may be noted.

The main aim of the book is to lay down rational procedures for the computer calculation of the performance of road vehicles. This, inevitably, involves empirical data that have to be obtained by experiment. The book therefore explains how these data may be obtained. To complete the work the book, in its later chapters, looks at automatic transmissions, both of conventional and unconventional designs, since these have a major effect on the determination of vehicle performance.

The chemical energy of the fuel in the tank of a vehicle is converted to a mechanical form of energy by the rather inefficient internal combustion engine. It is then dissipated by the forces opposing the motion of the vehicle, or vehicle drag. Chapter 1 therefore deals with the components of vehicle drag and their formulation. It is concerned mainly with the drag of road vehicles, but some indication of how the drag of "off-the-road" vehicles may be handled is included.

An indication of the values and the range of values of the coefficients of the drag equation are given in the first chapter. Chapter 2 sets out how these coefficients may be measured and gives details of the usual instrumentation employed.

If the performance of a vehicle is to be calculated at, say, the design stage, knowledge of the engine output must be obtained. The manner by which this is obtained is detailed in Chapter 3, together with the usual form of correction of engine power output, from that obtained on the day of the engine test to that which the engine can be expected to return on a day in which the ambient air pressure, temperature and humidity are stated, standard values. Techniques for the formulation of engine torque output for use in vehicle performance calculations are then described and discussed.

Before we can get down to the detail of the calculation of the performance of a vehicle there are certain loose ends to tie up. These are definitions of terms used in vehicle performance work such as "equivalent mass", "transmission efficiency", "gradient" and "the position of the centre of gravity", together with a number of contingencies which can occur during a test. One contingency is that, at the onset of a time-to-speed test, the wheels may lose some adhesion with the road. Another is that the vehicle, fortunately not the conventional motor car, may overturn in pitch. Such loose ends are dealt with in Chapter 4.

Chapter 5 sets out the algorithms for the calculation of the accelerative (time-to-speed) performance of a road vehicle with a manual transmission and for the calculation of the maximum speed of the vehicle on a straight level road. Such performance calculations for vehicles with conventional automatic transmissions are complicated by the fact that engine speed is not related to vehicle speed in a linear manner as there is a torque converter in the driveline. These then are left until Chapter 10, after the characteristics of the torque converter are dealt with and its match to the engine. These are covered in Chapter 9.

The definition of vehicle performance given in the second paragraph of this Introduction included fuel consumption. To calculate this entails knowledge of the engine characteristics not only throughout its speed range but also throughout its load range. Chapter 6 details how the engine is matched to the vehicle and its transmission and how the steady state fuel consumption may be calculated. This leads naturally to speculation on the benefits of a continuously variable transmission (CVT). Chapter 6 concludes by looking at the differences between the characteristics of the spark ignition, compression ignition, rotary and gas turbine engines.

A major advantage in being able to calculate the performance of a vehicle at the design stage, before any prototype has been built, is that parametric studies may be performed. That is, one particular design parameter, say vehicle weight or axle ratio, may be altered successively from a low extreme value to a high extreme value, and its effect noted. Chapter 7 sets out the results of the effect of altering the main parameters concerning the motor car and the commercial truck.

Before leaving manual transmissions, Chapter 8 looks at some reasons for fixing the number of gears and their ratio values. The techniques described are suitable for use in a computer program. Those for the ratios of the intermediate gears and for bottom gear are not the conventional techniques. In practice they rely heavily on the past experience of the designer, a process which makes it difficult to embody in the computer program being asked to make decisions.

Finally, Chapter 12 looks at some unconventional transmission systems of the continuously variable type designed to return very good fuel consumptions. These are designated shunt transmission because the power flow is carried from the engine to the wheels along two or more parallel paths. Calculation procedures for the main types of such shunt transmissions are set out in detail. Chapter 11 details the differential or torque splitting mechanism, an essential component of the shunt.

Road Vehicle Performance is intended to provide practising automotive engineers and students with the fundamental concepts of road vehicle performance, developed into workable, proven design techniques. The book ends with a bibliography to aid those working in the field. The references selected for inclusion are intended to give a flavour of the work on vehicle performance over the past twenty years. It is not intended to contain all the papers in the field. In general, the order of the bibliography follows the order of material in the book. Further references may be obtained from a study of the M.I.R.A. Abstracts, The Engineering Index and other abstracting authorities in the local library.

G.G. Lucas

1 Vehicle Drag

The term, vehicle drag, is used to describe the force resisting the motion of the vehicle and it is essential to know this in some detail for vehicle performance work. This force is a function, primarily, of vehicle speed but it is also affected by wind speed and ambient pressure and temperature. It need be evaluated for the straight-ahead vehicle motion only; it is not necessary for this work to consider the additional complications involved with cornering.

The drag force is a result of

(a) the deformation of the wheel

(b) the deformation of the ground

(c) the air flow over the vehicle

It is a sobering thought that the energy we have paid for in the fuel is all degraded into heating up the atmosphere through the engine exhaust, the engine coolant system, through turbulence caused by the displacement of air by the vehicle and through heat transfer from the transmission units and the tyres. After the passage of the vehicle the energy still remains, manifesting itself as a small temperature rise of the air, but it is impracticable to re-use it; effectively it is lost.

Conventionally, the term vehicle drag covers the force resisting motion due to the deformation of the wheel and the ground, the latter being negligible for vehicles on a normal road, and the drag force due to aerodynamic effects. Other loss paths, such as those due to the non-perfect efficiency of the transmission system and the wheel bearings, are covered by the use of a term known as the "transmission efficiency".

The Deformation of the Wheel

The pneumatic tyre is particularly suitable for use on road vehicles

1

because of its contribution to comfort, its excellent adhesion properties and because it does not break up the road surface to the extent of
a more rigid wheel. However, the vehicle load and tractive effort are
not carried without deformation. In the case of a pneumatic tyre on
the hard surface of a modern road, the deformation of the tyre
accounts for some 90-95% of the so-called "rolling" resistance of a
vehicle. Windage and slippage losses are small in comparison. The
distortion of the tread as it passes through the contact area results in a
hysteresis loss which manifests itself as heat and a rise in the temperature of the tyre. The term, rolling resistance, is the drag force of the
vehicle excluding that caused by aerodynamic effects. If this may be
considered as constant, it is the force necessary to push the vehicle at
low speed on flat level ground.

It is apposite here to differentiate between the two main types of
tyre construction. The radial ply tyre lays its tread squarely onto the
road with very little lateral constraint offered by the walls of the tyre.
This means that there is virtually no lateral slippage between tread
and road. However, the tread does bend as it passes through the
contact area. In the case of the cross ply tyre, the constraints offered
by the tyre walls cause distortion as the trend passes through the
contact area. This results in a hysteresis loss and a loss due to slippage
between tyre and road in the lateral direction. This difference
accounts for the lower rolling resistance and the superior wear and
fuel consumption characteristics of the radial ply tyre when compared
with the cross ply tyre.

Experience has shown that the rolling resistance, due to the hysteresis loss from the deformed tyre, is primarily a function of tyre deflection, that is of the load carried by tyre since the deflection is related to
the load. Other parameters affecting the rolling resistance of a
pneumatic tyre on a hard surface are tyre temperature, inflation
pressure, vehicle speed, tread thickness, the number of plies, the mix
of the rubber and the level of torque transmitted. These secondary
effects cannot be treated independently since there is some interaction. If the vehicle speed is increased and all other parameters are
maintained constant then the rolling resistance increases also. However, in practice, an increase in vehicle speed results in an increase in
tyre temperature and an increase in tyre pressure. Fortunately, as is
illustrated in Fig. 1.1, this interaction producing the higher pressure
and temperature detracts from the increase in rolling resistance due

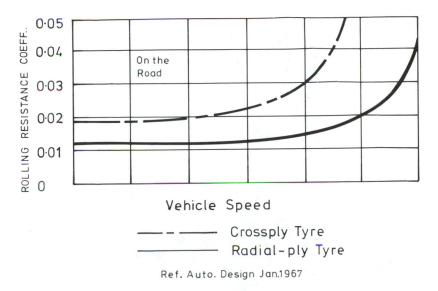

Vehicle Speed

— – — Crossply Tyre

——— Radial-ply Tyre

Ref. Auto. Design Jan.1967

FIGURE 1.1   Rolling Resistance

to speed, since both an increase in temperature and an increase in pressure have the effect of decreasing rolling resistance. The former because of the more supple nature of the rubber and the latter due to the decrease in the tyre deformation. The net result is, for a given tyre, a near constant rolling resistance with vehicle speed until such a speed is reached that a discernable standing wave sets in the tread in the wake of the contact area. Such a standing wave is shown in Fig. 1.2. The resistance to motion of the tyre increases very rapidly in this condition and the energy dissipated in the deformation caused by the standing wave is capable of destroying the tread in a very short time. It is usual therefore to quote a safe maximum speed for a particular tyre; well below the speed at which the standing wave sets in.

Since there is a direct relationship between the load on a tyre, the deflection and the hysteresis loss and since the load on all the wheels of a vehicle equals the vehicle weight it is usual to express the rolling resistance of a vehicle in terms of the non-dimensional rolling resistance coefficient

$$Ad = \text{rolling resistance } (Fd_{roll})/\text{vehicle weight } (W) \qquad 1.1$$

FIGURE 1.2

If the rolling resistance cannot be taken as constant throughout the speed range of the vehicle it is usual to add another coefficient, Bd, such that

$$\text{rolling resistance, } F_{d_{roll}} = W(Ad + Bd.V) \qquad 1.2$$

The tractive force transmitted by a tyre has a considerable effect on the rolling resistance. Within that area of tread in contact with the ground, the contact area, there are areas of micro-slip. The size of these areas increases as the tractive force transmitted increases thus increasing the energy loss and the resisting force. The rolling resistance of a tyre can be increased by a factor of 2 to 3 if transmitting a high tractive force.

Now, vehicle performance calculations are usually conducted at the full throttle condition where the torque level is high and fairly constant throughout the lower vehicle speed range where the rolling resistance is important. The rolling resistance coefficient(s) used therefore should be at the appropriate torque level.

In the absence of good experimental data it is usual to take $Bd = 0$ in expression 1.2 and to use the value of Ad given by the table below.

TABLE 1.1
ROLLING RESISTANCE COEFFICIENT (Ad)

	Cross ply	Radial ply
Car tyres	0.018	0.013
Truck and giant tyres	0.009	0.006
Earth moving tyres	0.014	0.008

The Deformation of the Ground

There are two cases to be considered here and both concern the operation of a vehicle on a surface other than a hard road. The first is where the ground may be considered "elastic", that is that the wheel of the vehicle deforms the ground which then returns back to its original condition after the vehicle has passed. The second is where the ground is softer and may be considered "plastic", that is that a permanent rut is left after the passage of the vehicle.

Fig. 1.3 depicts the case of a rigid wheel on an elastic surface. The ground in front of the moving wheel is heaped up and flows from the front, under and around the wheel, to the rear culminating in an energy loss and a rolling resistance. The effect of this on the wheel is to position the resultant (F) of the normal forces at some point A. Resolving the resultant (F) into its vertical and horizontal components; the vertical component must equal the load (W) on the wheel from equilibrium considerations and the horizontal component constitutes the rolling resistance force. Taking moments about the centre 0 of the wheel produces the result

$$\text{rolling resistance} = \frac{W.AB}{OB} = W.Ad \qquad 1.3$$

where again, Ad is the rolling resistance coefficient, found from experimental data.

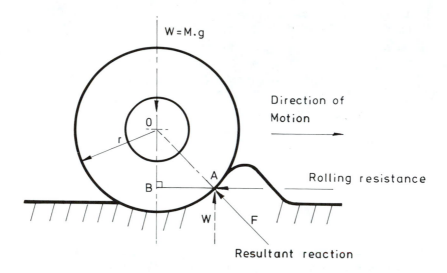

FIGURE 1.3   Wheel on 'soft' ground

However, the experimental data is not nearly so profuse as in the case of an elastic wheel on hard ground and there is the added difficulty that there is far greater variation in elastic ground characteristics than in elastic tyre characteristics. Fortunately, the deformation of the ground is insignificant for a normal vehicle tyre on a hard road and only comes into prominence in certain cross country cases. In such cases, special experiments must be conducted in order to determine the rolling resistance coefficient on the lines outlined in Chapter 2.

Consider now the case of a rigid wheel on ground which is not elastic. The ground deforms but does not return to its original condition after the wheel has passed. If the ground is wholly plastic, an energy balance yields the simple result that

the rolling resistance = b.p.z   1.4

where   b is the width of the rut
          p is the normal pressure between the wheel and the ground
and   z is the depth of sinkage

There is experimental evidence suggesting that this expression is valid.

In order to evaluate expression 1.4 it is necessary to know the normal pressure (p). This can be related to the sinkage (z) by

$$p = \left\{ \frac{k_c}{b} + k_\varnothing \right\} z^n \qquad\qquad 1.5$$

where   n = the sinkage exponent
k_c = the cohesive sinkage modulus
and $k_\varnothing$ = the friction sinkage modulus.

These three parameters are all properties of the soil. This expression has been developed for the case of a flat plate penetrating plastic ground but is used for the case of vehicle wheels also.

Using the relationship:—

Vehicle weight = p x projected contact area under the wheels   1.6

both p and z, and hence the rolling resistance can be found since the projected contact area under the wheel is a function of the sinkage (z).

This means that the case of a rigid wheel in plastic ground has to be treated differently to the two cases above. It is no longer sufficient to say that the rolling resistance is proportional to vehicle weight. The relationship between rolling resistance and vehicle weight is more complex and requires a detailed knowledge of the soil or ground material in the form of the three parameters n, k_c and $k_\varnothing$.

The Air Flow over the Vehicle

The moving vehicle, in displacing the surrounding air, has a resultant resisting force, termed the aerodynamic drag, imposed upon it. It is usual to express this drag non-dimensionally using the aerodynamic drag coefficient.

$$Cd = \frac{\text{Aerodynamic drag force}}{\frac{1}{2}.\rho.v^2 \times \text{a characteristic area}} \qquad\qquad 1.7.$$

where ρ = air density, usually taken as 1.23 kg/m^3
and v   = vehicle speed (m/s) relative to the air.
In order to nominate a suitable characteristic area it is as well to study the composition of the aerodynamic drag in rather more detail.

It is made up from the sum of three separate types of aerodynamic effects. These are:-

1. The air flow in the boundary layer resulting in the loss of momentum of the main stream. This effect produces the "skin friction" drag.
2. A component from the downwash of the trailing vortices behind the vehicle, resulting in the "induced" drag.
3. The "normal pressure" drag which may be found by the integration of the product (normal pressure × area) around the vehicle. This produces a net force opposing the motion of the vehicle because the separation of flow at the rear of the vehicle results in a lowering of the pressure on the rearward facing surfaces.

The skin fraction drag and the induced drag are usually small in relation to the normal pressure drag. However the skin friction drag can reach significant proportions in the case of a long vehicle, such as a coach. Since the major contributor to the aerodynamic drag is the normal pressure drag, the relevant characteristic area is the "projected frontal" area (A) of the vehicle. That is the area enclosed by the outline of the vehicle when viewed from the front.

The usual method of measuring this for an existing vehicle, if the drawings are not available, is to photograph the vehicle from the front. In order to approximate to the true projected frontal area it is necessary for the camera to be about 100 m from the vehicle and to use a telephoto lens fitted to the camera preferably having a focal length of at least 200 mm. Fig. 1.4 contains such a photograph taken with a 230 mm lens which may be compared with the adjoining photograph taken with the more usual 50 mm lens. The error involved in using the latter may be clearly seen. In the absence of suitable photographic equipment the projected frontal area may be estimated using the relationship.

$$A \simeq 0.8 \text{ (vehicle height above ground level × body width)} \qquad 1.8$$

FIGURE 1.4(a)

FIGURE 1.4(b)

However, such an approximate expression is no real substitute for a precise measurement and its use should be avoided.

The aerodynamic drag coefficient (Cd) for a particular vehicle is substantially a constant if side wind effects are ignored. A typical figure would be within the range 0.25 to 0.7. A vehicle having no attempt whatever at streamlining in its design such that, aerodynamically, it constitutes a "flying brick", would have an aerodynamic drag coefficient of approximately 0.8. However, aerodynamic drag coefficient values greater than unity may be realised with very long vehicles, such as trains. This is the influence of the skin friction drag.

The aerodynamic drag coefficient has been measured for a large number of vehicles by The Motor Industry Research Association (M.I.R.A.) and their findings have been published in a series of reports entitled "An experimental survey of vehicle aerodynamic characteristics". A sister report, entitled "A rating method for assessing vehicle aerodynamic drag coefficients", enables a Designer to assess the aerodynamic drag coefficient of his new vehicle.

The total drag force of a vehicle on a flat level road may be expressed by

$$Fd_{level} = W(Ad + Bd.V) + Cd.\tfrac{1}{2}.\rho.A.(V + Vw)^2 \qquad 1.9$$

where Ad, Bd and Cd are the drag coefficients

W = M.g = vehicle weight
ρ = air density (1.23 kg/m^3)
A = projected frontal area
V = vehicle speed

Vw is the "head-on" component of the wind speed provided that the wind speed is low and at a small angle only to the head-on direction. Any substantial component of wind speed in the yaw direction produces an additional drag force which complicates matters considerably.

2 Vehicle Performance Test Techniques

Much can be achieved in vehicle performance work with simple equipment. For a time-to-speed check on a vehicle the instrumentation may be as simple as a stop watch and a calibrated speedometer. The main drawback being in finding a suitable test surface or track. For accelerative performance this should be at least 1 km. long and preferably 2 km. It must be flat and level. It is difficult to find such a surface on the public road system and, when one can be found, it is not easy to conduct a test without causing inconvenience to other road users. Occasionally one finds a suitable track on a disused airfield but the ideal is a properly constructed track, such as one of those which exist at the proving ground of the Motor Industry Research Association near Nuneaton, England.

Occasionally, a route which simulates a particular driving pattern is required. A route which comprises bends, junctions and gradients, thus necessitating gear changes. Such a route can take account of the transient behaviour in vehicle performance, but it is very difficult to show conclusively that the particular route selected, which must of necessity be relatively simple, represents accurately a particular pattern of vehicle movement in real life. The vehicle manufacturers use such test routes, the aim being to ensure that their vehicle will live up to expectations and meet legislation requirements. Their proving grounds may comprise one or a number of these test routes.

It is possible also to model a test route, such that it may be followed in the laboratory on a chassis dynamometer. Here the vehicle drive-wheels are placed on rollers which are connected to a dynamometer; a power absorption and measurement device. Although the vehicle remains in-situ in the laboratory it may be made to perform as though it were on the road. The air flow through the engine cooling system may be provided by an external fan and load applied by the dynamometer to simulate the vehicle drag and a gradient. Inertia masses are usually bolted to the rotating shaft of the dynamometer to correctly simulate the mass of the vehicle. Hence the vehicle on the chassis dynamometer accelerates as it would on the road. Such a chassis dynamometer is depicted in Fig. 2.1. The driver may be provided with a monitor of his performance and the performance he is expected to achieve. This is usually arranged on a display screen in front of the vehicle; a very desirable adjunct to a driver attempting to follow a set driving pattern.

Simulations of this kind are finding a use in vehicle performance

FIGURE 2.1   Chassis dynamometer (some floor plates removed to show some of the machinery below)

work. Their drawback is that the simulations are of a relatively simple nature and may not represent adequately the pattern in the field. However, they are being used extensively in other related work. The legislation on exhaust pollution and fuel consumption requires that a particular simulation of urban driving pattern be followed on a chassis dynamometer in order that measurements may be made.

In vehicle performance work, it is important to ensure that the vehicle is being tested and not the driver and the vehicle. For instance, a driver may deliberately slip the clutch in order to make a smooth take-off of the vehicle from rest. One driver may slip the clutch more than another, so returning a different time-to-speed. In order to eliminate such driver effects a precise test procedure should be specified. This could be, for the above case, that the engine speed is held at some arbitrary and high value and, at the start of the test, the driver is instructed to slide his foot off the clutch pedal thereby engaging the clutch in a very short, and repeatable time. A similar technique could be followed when testing a vehicle having an automatic transmission. One could instruct the driver to depress both the accelerator and the brake pedal and to slide his foot off the brake pedal on the signal to start the test. Such techniques are desirable if reasonable repeatability of results is required.

The main parameters to be measured in vehicle performance work are vehicle speed, fuel consumption and the torque transmitted down the drive-line. In order to predict the performance of a vehicle the output from the engine must be known in some detail. This is best achieved by placing the engine upon a test bed and by conducting detailed measurements of engine torque output and fuel consumption against engine speed.

Other measurements, concerning the drag of the vehicle, involve the use of wind tunnels, tyre rigs and tow-dynamometers. Further, subsidiary tests may be necessary to determine the inertia of components and the mechanical efficiency of the transmission units. This chapter is concerned with the techniques for such measurements.

Vehicle Speed

It has been mentioned above that the vehicle's speedometer may be used to give a measure of the speed of the vehicle, but the instrument must be carefully calibrated. The readings themselves are not sufficiently accurate for vehicle performance purposes. It is not only the tolerances of mass production manufacture which produces an error. The amount of wear on the tyres also has an effect. The usual method of calibration is to drive the vehicle at set indicated speeds and time its progress over known distances. In this way the true speed may be determined and, by using a number of indicated speeds throughout the vehicle speed range, a graph of true speed against indicated speed may be drawn.

The determination of a set distance may present a problem depending upon one's locale. In Britain, the emergency telephones on the motorways are positioned a set distance apart, usually one mile, with this distance further subdivided into perhaps 8 or 16 subdivisions by subsidiary marker posts. Frequently when timing a vehicle at a set speed on the public roads the test is baulked by traffic conditions but, in the absence of other vehicles, one can hold a vehicle's speed sensibly constant over several miles and so compute the true speed. In the absence of existing distance marks it is necessary to use a surveyor's chain or a pedometer to mark out the distance. The timing device should ideally be a stop-watch.

The difficulty of trying to read a watch and a speedometer simultaneously may be overcome by arranging a camera to photograph both together. The camera must have some quick mechanism for winding on to the next frame since readings should be taken every second or so. However, such a complication is rarely necessary.

The more usual device in vehicle speed measurement is termed a "fifth wheel". This, as can be seen in Fig. 2.2, is clamped onto the rear of the vehicle and towed. By the use of such a carefully pre-calibrated instrument the necessity to calibrate every time it is used on another vehicle is avoided. The device consists of a wheel of low inertia (a bicycle wheel is sometimes used) mounted in a frame through low friction bearings. The frame is pivoted in two planes and its mounting bracket is clamped to the vehicle. The wheel may therefore move up and down and from side to side. A spring is arranged to pull the wheel onto the ground and a shock absorber is provided to damp out the bounce motions of the wheel. Since a low inertia, low friction wheel is used it is not too serious a matter if the wheel loses contact with the ground momentarily provided that the vehicle speed

FIGURE 2.2   FJH wheel

is not changing too rapidly. Braking tests and the like therefore may present a problem.

The speed signal from the fifth wheel may be arranged to be in analogue or digital form, or both. The analogue form may be provided by arranging that the fifth wheel drives a small electrical alternator. If a bicycle wheel is to be used as the fifth wheel, a hub type dynamo is suitable. The open circuit voltage across the terminals is virtually linear with speed. The analogue signal therefore takes the form of a volt meter; that is a needle on a calibrated dial, very similar in appearance to a speedometer.

A method more suited to sophisticated instrumentation is to arrange for an inductive transducer, or a light and phototransistor, to "look" at the periphery of a toothed disc rotating with the wheel. Every time a tooth (or a tooth space) passes the transducer an electrical pulse is induced in the cable from the transducer. This may then be converted to an analogue signal and/or, if further data processing is to occur in the laboratory, may be stored in some suitable device as pulses. If the data are to be recorded in this way there is considerable merit in storing the data as pulses because the need to calibrate, necessary if stored in analogue form, is avoided.

The use of measurement techniques of greater sophistication than the stop watch and speedometer demands that the accumulating data be recorded by the use of some instrumentation device. Such a device may be an ultra-violet recorder or an instrumentation magnetic tape recorder or a data logger in which the analogue signal input is converted to a digital signal in a form suitable for processing by computer. An ultra-violet recorder, in which the analogue signal input causes a beam of ultra-violet light to deflect across a moving strip of sensitive paper, may not be the most suitable instrument because the sensitive galvanometer may be disturbed by the vibrations of the vehicle and because the extraction of the data from the record can be a long and tedious process. A multi-channel tape recorder having mixed FM and DR capability and built to an instrumentation standard is a more robust piece of equipment. One channel may be used as a speech channel; a very useful facility in that comments may be made during the test which are recorded in synchronism with the recorded data. Perhaps the main advantage of a tape recorder however is that the recorded signals may be played back through analysis equipment in the laboratory so eliminating the tedious business of measuring ordinates on a strip of paper and the subsequent calculation or data handling procedure. A signal recorded on magnetic tape may be played back through a data logger for further processing by a digital computer.

A data logger is essentially a device which receives each analogue signal in turn and converts it into digital notation on, say, paper tape or in some other form such as magnetic tape or floppy disc suitable to be fed into a digital computer for further processing. The progress of electronics has been such that it is now possible for the analogue to digital (A to D) converter of the data logging equipment to be sufficiently small and portable to be contained within the vehicle. The signals may be stored in digital form on a very cheap magnetic tape deck. Unsophisticated arrangements, employing 47.5 mm/s ($1^7/8''$ per second) tape cassettes are being used. Such recording arrangements are small and robust. They are best used however in conjunction with a compatible mini-computer or main frame machine in the laboratory in order to process the collected data to the best advantage.

On permanent test grounds having well laid out test tracks and adequate instrumentation facilities it is possible to employ the Doppler Radar principle without any modification to the vehicle. A narrow beam radar dish of some 2 meters in diameter may be assembled at one end of the test track such that the speed of a vehicle on the test track may be monitored in much the same way as the radar check device used by the police, except that the installation is larger in order to cope with the larger distance.

Fuel Consumption

To measure the instantaneous fuel flow rate consumed by the engine is not an easy matter, particularly with a spark ignition engine, because the fuel flow rate into the carburettor may not equal the flow rate to the engine at any particular time. However, it is possible to measure the average fuel flow rate over a short period of time, say a few seconds.

A suitable instrument is of the positive displacement type. It consists of two main components, a metering unit which is placed in the fuel line between the supply tank of the vehicle and the engine and an indicator which is conveniently located where it can be seen by the test operators. The metering unit, typically, consists of two small chambers each containing fuel and each may be connected either to the input pipe from the fuel tank or to the outlet pipe to the engine depending upon the position of a solenoid operated slide valve. The two chambers are separated by a flexible diaphragm. As fuel is delivered to the engine from the first of the small chambers the diaphragm is displaced until it reaches the extremity of its stroke. At this point, which corresponds to a fixed and known amount of fuel, an electrical contact is made which causes the solenoid to change over the fuel connections to the two chambers and to cause the digital recorder in the indicator unit to notch on one unit. The second chamber then delivers fuel to the engine and, when the diaphragm reaches the other extremity of its stroke, again an electrical contact is made causing the solenoid valve to change over the connections and to record another unit on the indicator. The electrical supply for the instrument is the normal D.C. supply of the vehicle.

The calibration of the instrument is fixed by the size of the small chambers and is arranged by the manufacturer to give a convenient number of "clicks" per litre, say 500. In use, the operator resets the indicator to zero and, at the start of the test, he switches on the instrument and a stop-watch simultaneously. After a suitable period of time the indicator and stop-watch are switched off and the average fuel flow rate during the time interval computed.

Alternatively, instead of using the instrument in conjunction with a stop-watch, the odometer in the vehicle may be used to provide the fuel consumption rate in km per litre instead of litres per second.

Moments of Inertia of Rotating Parts

The weight of a vehicle is easy to measure if one has access to a weighbridge; and there is usually a public weighbridge not too far away. Alternatively, one may use a load cell to measure the reaction on each of the wheels in contact with the ground. The sum of these readings will give the vehicle weight. Knowledge of the vehicle mass is necessary in any performance calculation, since energy is stored in the moving mass in the form of kinetic energy.

However, knowledge of the mass of the vehicle itself is not enough, because, within the vehicle, there are shafts and wheels rotating at speed which also possess kinetic energy. The inertias of these rotating parts should also be known in order to provide the "equivalent" mass of the vehicle.

Perhaps the most important rotating inertia is that of the engine, particularly when a low gear is engaged. As a rule-of-thumb guide, the equivalent mass of the engine of a motor car when in bottom gear is similar to the mass of the vehicle. Its importance however diminishes rapidly as the higher gear ratios are engaged. Other rotating inertias include the road wheels and those of the drive train.

The most usual laboratory technique for the measurement of such inertias is the use of the trifilar suspension system, as described below. This may be applied quite readily in the case of the wheels since it is usually not too difficult to find a wheel similar if not identical to the wheel in question to place on a trifilar suspension rig. The importance of the Cardan shaft inertia is not too great such that it may be estimated from drawings with sufficient accuracy. The difficulty is the engine inertia. This may be determined quite readily by the trifilar suspension method but it requires that the engine be dismantled in order that the rotating parts (the flywheel, clutch and crankshaft assembly) may be mounted on the trifilar suspension. This is not always convenient.

If the accuracy of the vehicle performance calculations is not of paramount importance, as may be the case if it is intended to conduct parametric studies, it may be sufficient to estimate the polar moment of inertia of the engine rotating parts. The majority of this inertia is due to the flywheel and clutch assembly. Now, the polar moment inertia of the clutch assembly may be obtained from the clutch manufacturer and the flywheel may usually be treated as a disc having a heavy rim. The central web, of radius r_1, may be said to have a polar moment of inertia of its mass, M_1, multiplied by its (radius of gyration)^2

i.e. $$I_1 = \frac{M_1 r_1^2}{2}$$ 2.1.

The heavy rim, having an inner radius of r_1, an outer radius of r_2 and a mass M_2, may be said to have polar moment of inertia

$$I_2 = \frac{M_2(r_2^2 - r_1^2)}{2}$$ 2.2.

The total polar moment of inertia therefore of the rotating parts of the engine may be estimated to be

$$I_e = I_{clutch} + I_1 + I_2 + (10\% \text{ to } 15\% \text{ to cater for the crankshaft assembly})$$ 2.3.

A trifilar suspension system suitable for the measurement of the polar moment of inertia of rotating parts consists of a low inertia platform suspended on three equally spaced vertical wires. The platform is conveniently arranged to have a central hole and should lie in the horizontal plane. The inertia of the platform itself may be determined by setting the system vibrating in the torsional mode about the central vertical centre-line. Timing the system to swing through, say, 15 complete oscillations enables the time (t_d) for one complete oscillation, or the periodic time, to be determined. The polar moment of inertia of the platform is then given by

$$I_d = M_d. \left[\frac{r^2}{4\pi^2} \times g \times \frac{t_d^2}{l} \right]$$ 2.4.

where M_d = the mass of the platform

r = the radius at which the wires lie from the vertical centre-line of the system

g = the acceleration due to gravity

and l = the length of the wires

Repeating the experimental exercise with a mass (M), say a crank-shaft and flywheel assembly, positioned centrally on the platform produces a new periodic time (t). Note that the crankshaft may pass through the central hole of the platform.

The polar moment of inertia of the mass (M) then is calculable from

$$I = \left[\frac{r^2}{4\pi^2} (M_d + M)g \times (\frac{t^2}{l}) \right] - I_d$$ 2.5.

The radius (r) of the assembly should be such that it is possible to measure the polar moment of inertia of quite large diameter assemblies, such as the road wheels of a vehicle. The three wires must be vertical in the neutral or central position of the platform and, when the system is being vibrated, there should be no displacement in the lateral direction.

The accuracy of the measurement may be improved if the experiment is repeated with several different lengths (l) of the suspension wires. Since there exists a linear relationship between t^2 and the wire length (l), the slope of a graph of t^2 against l may be used instead of t^2/l in expression 2.5. The plotting of this straight line reduces the scatter on the experimental results and so improves the accuracy of the measurement.

Frequently, in vehicle performance work, the situation arises where calculations are to be carried out upon the performance of an existing vehicle. In such case it may be inconvenient to remove and strip down the engine in order to measure its polar moment of inertia. Little inconvenience would be caused however by the removal of a wheel in order to measure its polar moment of inertia. It may be of advantage therefore to be capable of measuring the engine inertia in situ. This may be achieved by the following technique developed by The Rover Co. Ltd.

The engine is prevented from rotating by a special sprag device manufactured for the purpose. This is inserted through one of the inspection holes in the clutch housing and clamps the flywheel by engaging into the starter ring teeth. The procedure then is to engage second gear and, with the brakes fully released, to tow the vehicle along a level floor with a force of up to 1800 N ($\simeq$ 400 lbf) and to measure the movement of the vehicle. This may then be repeated in the reverse direction, the force versus movement data forming a hysteresis loop, the mean slope of which is a measure of transmission stiffness.

The engine may now be released by the removal of the sprag and the vehicle fitted with an accelerometer placed near the centre of gravity or some other device to measure the drive-line natural frequency. Driving the vehicle in second gear along a smooth road and the sudden opening of the throttle causes the fundamental mode of the drive-line torsional natural frequency to be excited. This mode consists of the engine inertia connected to the inertia of the vehicle through the transmission stiffness just measured and its natural frequency is registered in the output from the accelerometer and may be recorded on a U-V recorder or on magnetic tape for subsequent measurement.

The equivalent mass of the vehicle may be assessed as being the mass of the vehicle plus the equivalent inertia of the road wheels, thus

$$M_E = M_v + \frac{I_w}{r_r^2} \qquad\qquad 2.6.$$

where M_v = vehicle mass, I_w = the total polar moment of inertia of the road wheels and r_r = the rolling radius of the road wheels.

The substitution of this into the expression linking the measured natural frequency (f) with the inertias and the connecting stiffness of a two mass, one spring system, viz

$$f = \frac{1}{2_\pi} \sqrt{\frac{S(M_E + I_e \cdot g_x{}^2)}{(M_E \cdot I_e \cdot g_x{}^2)}} \qquad\qquad 2.7.$$

enables the engine inertia (I_e) to be determined. In the above expression, S is the stiffness as measured by the tow test described above and g_x is defined as

$$g_x = \frac{g_a \cdot g_g}{r_r} \qquad\qquad 2.8.$$

where g_a = drive axle ratio, g_g = gearbox ratio and r_r = the rolling radius of the drive wheels.

The use of this technique may be criticised on the grounds that the vehicle inertia is not correctly represented and that the stiffness includes some deflection of the engine mountings, nevertheless the correlation between this method and a more rigorous method has been found to be good.

Transmitted Torque

Occasionally it is necessary to measure the torque transmitted down the drive-line of a vehicle. This is not a straight forward procedure because it usually involves the extraction of a signal from rotating parts. On rigs in the laboratory it is sometimes possible to arrange the design such that a drive unit may be mounted in gimbals and a measure of the transmitted torque obtained by measuring the torque reaction on the casing of the unit. However, it is usually not possible to arrange this in vehicle test work.

The usual method of measuring torque is to strain-gauge a suitable shaft in the drive-line system. One such shaft may be the input to the gearbox shaft, sometimes termed the gearbox first motion shaft. Fig. 2.3 shows this shaft equipped for the measurement of torque. Four active strain-gauges have been fitted at 45° to the axis of the shaft (only two can be seen however in Fig. 2.3, the other two are positioned in a symmetrical manner on the other side of the shaft). By so arranging, temperature and shaft bending signals can be eliminated and the four active strain-gauges provide a strong signal related to torque. Fig. 2.3 shows also four copper slip-rings cemented onto the

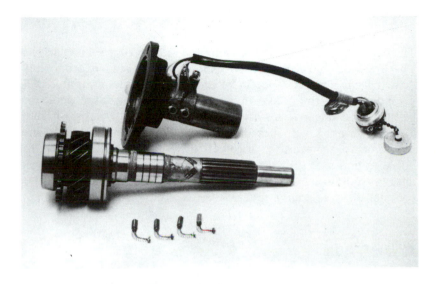

FIGURE 2.3

shaft and the front bearing housing of the gearbox extended to house the brushes for the slip-rings. Two slip-rings carry the electrical power into and out of the strain-gauge bridge while the other two carry the bridge signal for remote recording. This system works well provided that oil can be prevented from contaminating the slip-rings.

An alternative arrangement is to replace the slip-ring assembly with a telemetry system for the transmission of the strain-gauge signal from the rotating shaft. This may take the form of a radio telemetry system employing capacitive coupling aerial systems in order to suppress radiation or, alternatively, the data may be transmitted over a distance of a few inches between rotor and stator by means of a magnetic coupling. A particular feature of the latter system is that it lends itself to permanent, or semi-permanent installations, since it can be powered externally. Also, several units may be operated in close proximity without interaction. Another method of measuring the torque transmitted down the drive-line of a vehicle is to employ a specially designed strain-gauged member which can be fitted between the drive wheels and the axle flange. Such devices are available as proprietary units and can be adapted to suit different vehicles.

Vehicle Drag

The drag force, or the force resisting the motion of a vehicle may, as we have seen in Chapter 1, be expressed as a second order polynomial having vehicle speed (V) as the independent variable. The second order term is known as the aerodynamic drag while the constant and linear terms are together called the rolling resistance. The two terms may be measured separately in different test facilities or they may be measured together in a vehicle test known as the "deceleration test". We shall take the measurement of rolling resistance first followed by the measurement of aerodynamic drag and then consider the deceleration test.

Rolling Resistance

There are two methods in current use for the determination of the rolling resistance of a tyre. The first is to enclose the test wheel within a frame, the wheel being mounted on an axle and free to rotate, and to tow the assembly behind a vehicle. The rolling resistance may be measured by incorporating a load measuring device in the towbar. Weights may be placed in panniers fixed to the sides of the frame in order to place a vertical load on the wheel.

When designing such a tow-box it is desirable to incorporate the provision for setting different camber angles and for setting the wheel in planes other than the straight ahead. Then, by the provision of load cells to measure forces in the other directions, a useful general purpose tyre test facility is provided. The main disadvantage in using such a rig for the measurement of tyre rolling resistance is that there may be little control over the road surface in use or in the temperature of the tyre.

The second method of measurement is to load the test wheel against a rotating drum of large diameter. This type of rig is usually preferred to the tow-box because a closer control can be made of the operating conditions. Allowance has to be made for the fact that the tyre is in contact with a curved rather than a flat surface when interpreting the results.

Fig. 2.4 shows a typical drum test rig. The drum is driven by a

FIGURE 2.4   Tyre drum test rig. (Courtesy of Goodyear Tires, Luxembourg)

motor and the forces on the wheel are measured by the use of an instrumented hub.

Aerodynamic Drag

The usual method of obtaining the aerodynamic drag co-efficient of a vehicle is to subject either the vehicle itself or a model to wind tunnel tests. These tests however pose certain difficulties which may be classified under four headings.

a) The correct representation of the ground

b) Blockage effects

c) The correct representation of the vehicle

d) Reynold's number effects; that is the correct flow pattern over the model.

Points c) and d) may be avoided by the use of a full scale wind tunnel capable of taking the complete vehicle. Such a facility exists at the Motor Industry Research Association, near Nuneaton, England, and is capable of accepting quite large motor cars. It has the added advantage that a chassis dynamometer has been built into the floor of the working section capable of absorbing 250 horsepower. The vehicle under test therefore may be driven under load, the drive wheels driving rollers which are connected to a dynamometer to absorb the power. However, such test facilities are very expensive.

If a model of the vehicle is to be employed the scale should be as large as possible in order to approach the Reynold's number of the full size vehicle and it should faithfully represent the external features of the vehicle to within $\pm$ 2mm. Further, the degree of "roughness" on the underside of the vehicle, protuberances such as exhaust systems, axles etc., should be represented and provision made for the air flow through the engine cooling system. These models are usually made of wood and their manufacture is best entrusted to specialists. They are not cheap to produce and their cost may well be in the region of the cost of the full size vehicle itself.

A model placed in a wind tunnel of finite size results in the flow of air around the model being affected by the presence of the walls of the wind tunnel. This blockage effect, provided that the model is not too large, may be allowed for by the application of correction factors supplied by the manufacturer of the wind tunnel.

The correct representation of the ground however is difficult to deal with. On the road, the vehicle moves relative to the air and to the ground. In a wind tunnel the vehicle is stationary and so may have no velocity relative to the ground. There are several methods employed to overcome this problem.

The most usual is the endless belt method. Here the model is positioned in the wind tunnel with its wheels just clear of an endless belt moving at the air speed of the working section.

The model is arranged in the working section and attached to, usually, a three component balance capable of measuring lift, drag and pitching moment. For the determination of the aerodynamic drag coefficient however only the drag force measurement is required.

The Deceleration Test

This method has a great deal to recommend it because it requires no expensive rig facilities and because it is capable of providing both the aerodynamic drag and the rolling resistance coefficients. The main requirements are the vehicle itself, with simple instrumentation, and a long, straight, flat and level road; the latter usually being the most difficult to find. The vehicle under test is driven up to a speed approaching its maximum speed and is then allowed to coast to rest in neutral gear. The deceleration against vehicle speed data are collected during this coasting period either from deceleration measurements directly or, more usually, indirectly from a recording of vehicle speed against time data. The indirect method is favoured because to attempt to measure deceleration directly without very sophisticated equipment results in a great deal of "noise" on the signal from the decelerometer caused by the pitch of the vehicle and the vibration of the structure of the vehicle.

Fig. 2.5 contains the data from a deceleration test on a small motor car and is here used to illustrate the technique of obtaining the drag coefficients from such data. The first step is to determine slopes of the

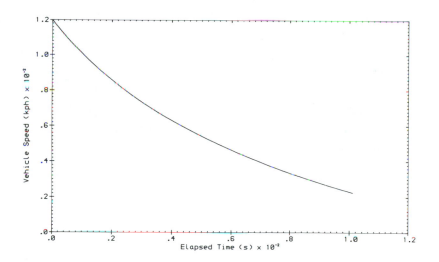

FIGURE 2.5   Coast-down data for small car

curve in Fig. 2.5 in order to obtain vehicle deceleration as a function of vehicle speed. This may be achieved by the drawing of tangents to the curve at a number of different vehicle speeds throughout the range or, better still, the fitting of a polynomial expression of, say, order six and differentiating the expression to give the required deceleration. A suitable curve fitting technique is the "method of least squares" which affords the coefficients a_0, a_1, a_2 etc., in the polynomial expression.

$$V = a_0 + a_1t + a_2t^2 + a_3t^3 + a_4t^4 + a_5t^5 + a_6t^6$$

V being vehicle speed and t being time.

By so fitting a polynomial any scatter on the data is smoothed out and the expression may be readily differentiated to give the deceleration. Thus the deceleration is

$$-\frac{dV}{dt} = -\left[a_1 + 2a_2t + 3a_3t^2 + 4a_4t^2 + 5a_5t^4 + 6a_6t^5 \right]$$

and may be evaluated at a number of discrete speeds throughout the vehicle speed range. Then, by the application of Newton's second law

$$\text{Force} = \text{Mass} \times \frac{dV}{dt}$$

the drag force on the vehicle is given by

$$F_d = W(A_d + B_d \cdot V) + \tfrac{1}{2}\rho A C_d V^2 = \left(M + \frac{I_w}{r_r^2}\right)\left(-\frac{dV}{dt}\right)$$

where   M = vehicle mass
         W = vehicle weight (=M.g)
         V = vehicle speed
         I_w = the total road wheel inertia
         r_r = the rolling radius of the road wheels
         ρ = air density
         A = the projected frontal area

and A_d, B_d and C_d are the drag coefficients.

If B_d may be considered zero, a plot of F_d against V^2 should yield a straight line, the slope of which equals $\frac{1}{2}.\rho.A.C_d$ and the intercept on the drag force axis equals $W.A_d$.

This technique may readily be extended to incorporate the effects of a slight head-on wind component on the day of the test and to yield the drag coefficients in the event that B_d cannot be considered zero.

It can be shown that, if B_d is small, the law of the velocity versus time curve of the deceleration test is

$$V = L \left[\frac{\dfrac{(V_o + n)}{L} - \text{Tan} \,(Z.L.t.)}{1 + \dfrac{(V_o + n)}{L} \, \text{Tan} \,(Z.L.t.)} \right] - n$$

where

$$L = \left| \frac{a}{c} - \frac{b^2}{4C^2} \right|^{1/2}$$

$$Z = \frac{C}{M_E}$$

and $n = b/2C$

This, together with an optimisation routine of the direct search type, can be used as an alternative method to extract the vehicle drag coefficients. The technique requires computing facilities, but is likely to be more accurate than the other method outlined above.

An alternative to the measurement of vehicle drag which may be applied to a new project at the design stage is the "rating" method developed by The Motor Industry Research Association*. Briefly the method involves the assessment of such features of the vehicle as the degree of roundness of the corners in the plan view, in the side eleva-

---

*White, R.G.S. "A method of estimating automobile drag coefficients" S.A.E. Paper No. 690189, 1969.

tion and in the front view, etc. against sets of sketches ranging from the very square to the well rounded. By choosing the sketches most resembling the features of the vehicle in question and manipulating the weighting factors provided in the prescribed manner, an estimation of the aerodynamic drag coefficient (C_d) may be made within a claimed accuracy of $\pm 7\%$.

3 Engine Power

The power delivered by the engine is transmitted down the drive-line of the vehicle to be translated into a propulsive force at the drive wheels. It is essential therefore for vehicle performance calculations that the engine characteristics are known in some detail. These are usually obtained by removing the engine from the vehicle and placing it on a test bed in the laboratory where more precise measurements may be made. Alternatively, the vehicle itself may be placed upon a chassis dynamometer.

The measurements so obtained are usually the steady state characteristics of the vehicle; that is they do not include such transient effects as the changes in torque and fuel consumption produced by an accelerating engine. Such changes from the steady state measurements may result in small differences in the fuel and air flow rates into the engine and hence in the power output. There will also be a difference caused by the engine having to accelerate its own inertia. This latter difference may be large but is easy to modify the steady state results to take this into account. The other transient effects are difficult to accommodate and, since they are small and the engine acceleration during a time-to-speed test is generally low, it is usual to ignore them.

Engine Test Beds

It is not possible here to deal in full with all the facilities available in a modern engine laboratory; simply to describe the equipment necessary for engine testing for vehicle performance work is all that is possible. For further study the reader is referred to more specialised books on the testing of internal combustion engines. Suffice it to say that the engine is mounted on a test bed and connected to a dynamometer which absorbs the power output from the engine and

31

gives a measure of the torque delivered by the engine. Built into the dynamometer is an instrument which measures the speed of the dynamometer shaft. The power output from the engine therefore is simply the product of torque and speed.

In addition to torque and speed measurements the other engine quantity which may require to be measured for vehicle performance purposes is the steady state fuel consumption. This may be achieved by use of the positive displacement device described in Chapter 2 or by a simple pipette and timer device. A three-way valve at the base of the pipette enables the engine to draw fuel from the main supply only, to fill the pipette or to draw from the pipette only so enabling the fuel flow rate to be measured by timing the passage of, say, 50 ml.

It is important that the engine under test be in full vehicle trim if meaningful vehicle performance calculations are to result. The engine must have its normal air cleaner system and be driving all its usual accessories, such as its fan, water pump, a charging alternator, oil pump etc. It is important also, although not always possible, that the exhaust system be very similar to the system installed on the vehicle. If the laboratory exhaust system has to be used it is usual to arrange that the pressure in the exhaust port of the engine is similar to that when installed in the vehicle. This, however, neglects the pronounced effect that standing waves in the exhaust system may have on engine performance.

Installation of the fan is not a difficult matter generally. This is fortunate since it can absorb 10 to 20% of the engine power output. There may be some difference in the cooling of the engine between its installed condition in the vehicle and that on the test bed. This can result in a small difference in the power to drive the water pump or fan but this usually is small. Again, the drive to the alternator is straightforward to arrange and, although the power involved is low, the alternator should be arranged to charge a battery or be connected to a small load. The air cleaner however, frequently removed from laboratory engines in order to improve accessibility, must be in situ since it can have a considerable effect on engine output. Fig. 3.1 shows the torque output from a 1.5 litre spark ignition engine with and without the air cleaner. Both curves were obtained within minutes of each other and show that the change in configuration of the inlet system, with its attendant change in the pressure wave system, may be more important than the introduction of a small

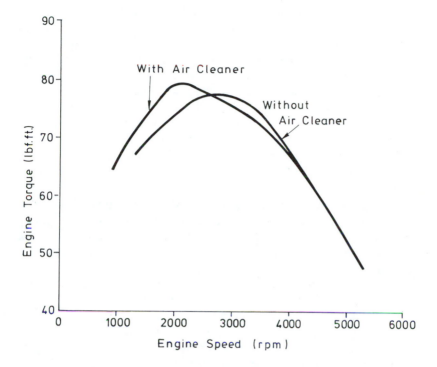

FIGURE 3.1   Effect of air cleaner on torque curve

pressure loss through the air cleaner.

An alternative to the engine test bed for the determination of the engine characteristic is the use of a chassis dynamometer. This is suitable, although not generally favoured, for the situation where the engine is already installed in the vehicle and it is inconvenient to remove it. Such a device is described in Chapter 2.

A chassis dynamometer has the obvious advantages of convenience and that the torque measured is that at the drive wheels. However, it is not so easy to control conditions when using a chassis dynamometer and the distortion of the drive wheel tyres can introduce problems. It is more usual therefore to use an engine test bed for the determination of engine characteristics.

The engine torque characteristics obtained must, of course, include the full throttle or full load torque against engine speed curve. This is necessary for the calculation of vehicle accelerative performance and maximum speed. If it is intended to conduct steady-state calculations at vehicle speeds lower than the maximum, such as the prediction of fuel consumption, it is necessary to obtain data throughout the engine load range. The parameter used to define an engine condition at other than the full load may be the throttle angle for a spark ignition engine or it may be the inlet manifold depression. Both are easy to measure. The former by a potentiometer if the engine is in situ in a vehicle or by a pointer and protractor if on a test bed. The latter by a differential pressure transducer or by a U-tube manometer.

Selection of which parameter to use as a measure of load is quite arbitrary. The fixed inlet manifold pressure has the advantage that numerically it is a better indication of load because the throttle angle depends so much upon the type of carburetter. Further, it is not easy to set the datum of zero throttle angle and a small error here can make an appreciable difference to the torque output, particularly at low throttle angles.

However, the above concerns the presentation of the character-istics. For their measurement it is almost always preferable to use fixed throttle positions and to run the engine over its speed range at each throttle setting. Then by recording inlet manifold pressure with engine torque and fuel consumption data, it is possible to cross-plot the results to give lines of torque against engine speed at a number of constant inlet pressure values.

The usual parameter to obtain a measurement of load on a compression ignition engine is the fuel pump rack position. However, when presenting graphs describing the performance of a compression ignition engine the measured data are usually reduced and cross-plotted to give engine brake mean effective pressure (b.m.e.p.) as the parameter describing load.

In order that such data may be meaningful, it is important to correct for ambient pressure and temperature and so present results appertaining to a "standard" day. In this way the results of one engine may be compared with those of another or the results of a particular engine related to atmospheric conditions different from those of the test day. There are a number of codes enabling one to correct engine performance results. These, generally, for the spark ignition engine, are based upon the factoring of the indicated power by the ratio of the standard dry ambient pressure to that of the observed and the square root of the ratio of observed ambient temperature to that of the standard temperature. Some justification for this is given by Greene, A.B. and Lucas, G.G. "The Testing of Internal Combustion Engines" English Universities Press, London, 1969, pages 133 to 135. Briefly, this justification attaches equal weighting to the effect of charge density and the ability of the engine to "breathe". Hence the square root sign over the temperature ratio.

Correction codes define the terms associated with engine testing and the level of accuracy required in the measurement of the test quantities. The British Standard Code (BS 5514, see also ISO 3046) corrects the engine measured power output of the normally aspirated spark ignition engine generally as outlined above. The correction of the measured power output of the compression ignition engine, however, has to be treated rather differently because, at part load, a fixed quantity of fuel is injected into excess air. The power output therefore is related to charge density. Similarly, turbo charging results in further changes to the code.

The procedure for the correction of specific fuel consumption figures for the effects of ambient conditions is not nearly so well defined. There may be expected to be some difference in this effect between an engine which has fuel injection and an engine which employs a carburettor. Some correction codes ignore the effect completely. The British Standard Code BS 5514 Part 1 1982 has a simple correction technique which uses the factors it advocates for the correction of power. However, it also leaves room for any other rational method to be used.

Fig. 3.2 shows the torque characteristics of a 1.6 litre spark ignition engine constructed from data taken with fixed throttle positions. For a study of vehicle performance it is usually desirable to present a picture of the engine power output against engine speed.

Now since power is torque × speed, the data in Fig. 3.2 may be used to provide Fig. 3.3. This shows the corrected power at the engine flywheel plotted against engine speed. Fig. 3.4 shows the corresponding specific fuel consumption curves.

The data in these latter two figures are best presented as one picture. This may be achieved by cross-plotting the s.f.c. curves of Fig. 3.4 onto Fig. 3.3. To do this, select a s.f.c. value, say 0.09 mg/J. Rule a horizontal line on Fig. 3.4 corresponding to this s.f.c. value and note the engine speed and throttle angle at each point it crosses a

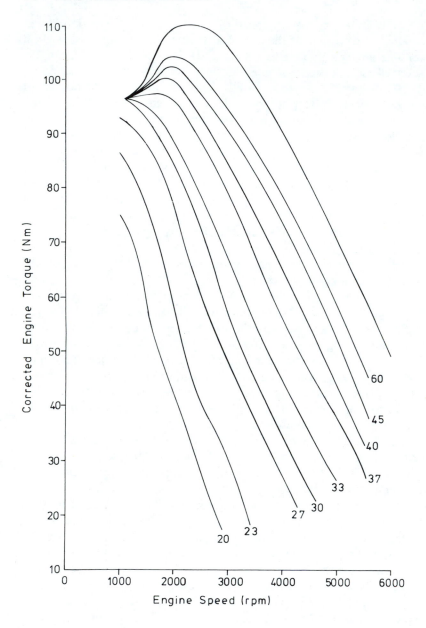

FIGURE 3.2   Engine torque curve (1.6l)

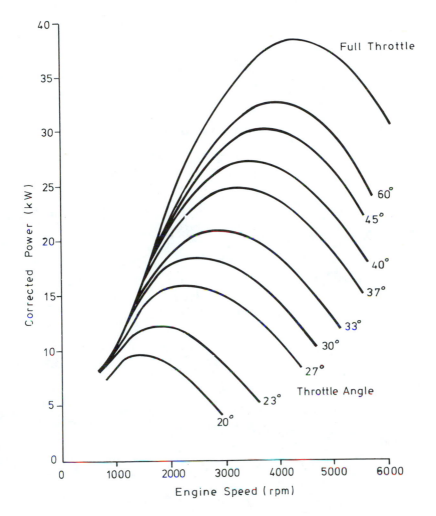

FIGURE 3.3   Engine power curves for 1.6l engine

constant throttle angle line. Then, by locating these points on Fig. 3.3 a contour of constant s.f.c. = 0.09 mg/J may be drawn. Repeating this procedure for a number of other constant s.f.c. values results in the combined power and specific fuel consumption characteristic shown in Fig. 3.5.

This shows at a glance the most economical running point of the

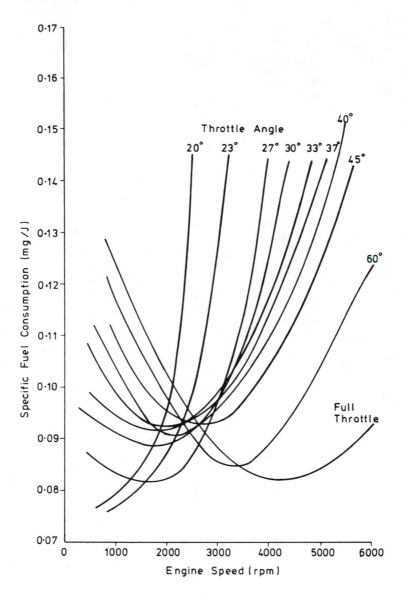

FIGURE 3.4   Specific fuel consumption of 1.6l engine

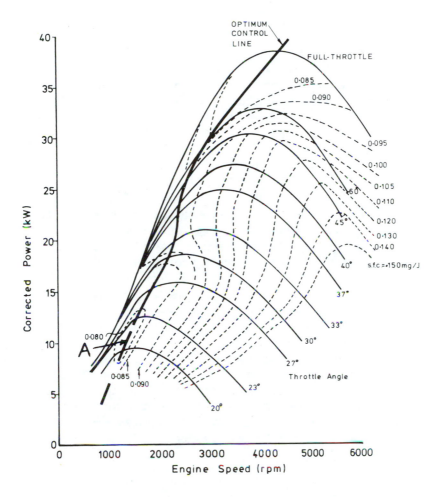

FIGURE 3.5   Characteristics of 1.6l engine

engine to be at point A, in the ce.   of the nest of specific fuel
consumption contours. If, however, the engine is to be of variable
speed rather than having a fixed speed the most economical manner
of operating the engine would be to control it along the "optimum
control line", shown in Fig. 3.5.

Having obtained the engine characteristics and presented them
graphically in a convenient form it is now necessary to consider their

use in vehicle performance calculations. It is shown in Chapter 6 that graphs of the form of Fig. 3.5 may be used in the prediction of the steady-state fuel consumption of a vehicle. For vehicle acceleration and maximum speed calculations however, the relevant data is the engine full load torque curve. If, as is now usual, a digital computer is to be employed in the conduction of such time-to-speed calculations the problem arises as to the most suitable description of the torque curve for use with a computer.

One may store in core or on file a matrix of engine torque and speed data and provide an interpolative subroutine to evaluate the engine torque at any desired intermediate engine speed value. This suffers from the obvious disadvantage of the large amount of numbers which must be handled in order to describe the torque curve and the attendant possibility of an error in the read-in data. A sub-routine to interpolate between data is necessary because the engine speed at which the vehicle performance computer program calls for the corresponding value of engine torque may not be one of the values fed in, but some intermediate speed between two of these values. The interpolative subroutine could assume a linear relation-ship between adjacent points if the read-in data is sufficiently close but it is likely that a second order polynomial or above subroutine may be necessary to obtain a sufficient standard of accuracy.

An alternative method having a great deal to recommend it is to fit some suitable mathematical expression to the engine torque data by, say, the "method of least squares". A suitable mathematical expres-sion being a polynomial since it is versatile and readily amenable to mathematical treatment. Such an expression would take the form

$$T_e = a_o + a_1 \left(\frac{N_e}{1000}\right) + a_2 \left(\frac{N_e}{1000}\right)^2 + a_3 \left(\frac{N_e}{1000}\right)^3 + \dots \text{ etc.} \qquad 3.4.$$

a_0, a_1, a_2, a_3 etc., being the polynomial coefficients determined from the curve fit. The independent variable is here shown to be engine speed (rev/min) divided by 1000. This is to avoid the handling of numbers of very large magnitude during the curve fit procedure and the attendant loss of accuracy.

Such a procedure will smooth out the original data and provide the coefficients a_0, a_1, a_2 etc., as the read-in data from which the vehicle performance program can generate the engine torque at any required engine speed. The form of the polynomial expression makes it suitable to be differentiated and equated to zero in order to establish the maximum torque speed. The coefficients may be factored in order to cater for the changes in torque output as a result of changes in ambient pressure and temperature.

The method of least squares is a very popular curve fit method and is described in standard works on curve fitting. A suitable computer program may be found in the libraries of most computer centres. Briefly the method arranges the curve, in this case described by a polynomial, such that the sum of the squares of the differences between it and the data points is a minimum. The square of the differences is used in order to give the same significance to both positive and negative differences.

Fig. 3.6 shows the fit of polynomial expressions of order 2, 3, 4 and 6 to a typical torque curve. The fit of the higher orders is well within the accuracy of the original curve. It is recommended therefore that a polynomial expression of order six is suitable for the description of an engine torque curve.

In using such an expression two points must be borne in mind. The first is that the data used to describe the torque curve should cover the full speed range of the engine. The reason for this is that the curve fitted will lie close to the data points within the speed range of the points. Outside this range the curve may take up a shape quite unrepresentative of an engine torque curve. In the absence of data points near the extremes of the engine speed range it is preferable to extrapolate the data to provide points.

Fig. 3.7 shows this danger by the fitting of a sixth order to the torque of a 1.5 litre racing engine from data over the speed range 3000 to 7500 rev/min. The circles denote the experimental points and the continuous line the fitted polynomial. This illustrates that, while the fit is excellent within the data range, to evaluate the polynomial at a speed above 7500 rev/min or below 3000 rev/min may lead to a considerable error in any subsequent calculations. If the engine may be required to operate in these regions there should be data points to constrain the polynomial curve fit.

The second point is not so serious. It concerns the number of data points. This number must be greater than 1 plus the order number of the polynomial, i.e. 7 points minimum for a sixth order polynomial. Ideally, it should be as high as possible to avoid the possibility of the

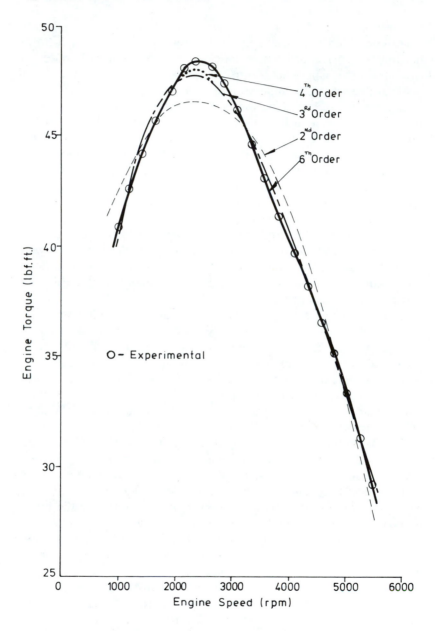

FIGURE 3.6   Polynomial curve fit to torque curve

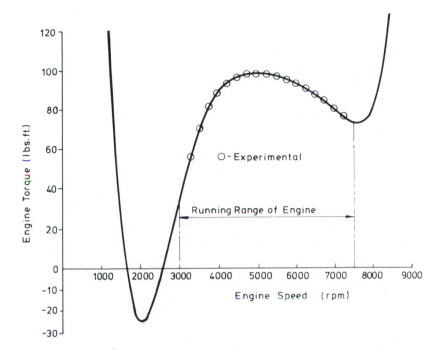

FIGURE 3.7   Polynomial curve fit to torque curve of a 1.6l racing engine

curve wandering off course in between data points. In practice, fifteen to forty points has been found to be satisfactory for the fitting of a sixth order polynomial.

In conclusion therefore, the engine torque output may be measured on a dynamometer test bed or a chassis dynamometer and may be described suitable for use in a vehicle performance program by a polynomial expression or by the storage of data points within a matrix and the use of an interpolative subroutine.

4 Miscellaneous Vehicle Performance Parameters

In order to carry out effective vehicle performance calculations, techniques have to be developed to cater for a number of miscellaneous contingencies. We have mentioned already the convenience of expressing the rotational inertias, together with the mass of the vehicle, as an equivalent vehicle mass. The formulation of this is detailed below. Another important consideration is the power loss down the drive-line, or transmission efficiency. This requires some care in the manner in which it is expressed because it can have a considerable influence on the resulting calculated time-to-speed of a vehicle.

The gradient, or slope upon which a vehicle is moving is an environmental parameter for which there exists a number of descriptions. Associated with movement on a gradient is the need to describe the behaviour of the vehicle during the "take-off" period; those first few seconds as a vehicle moves from rest. This, in its turn raises the possibility of the occurrence of "wheel-spin"; that phenomenon characteristic of high performance motor cars in which the drive wheels lose their grip on the ground, causing relative motion between tyre tread and the ground. The phenomenon is not the sole prerogative of the high performance car however, it can occur with vehicles of very modest performance on steep gradients and/or on slippery terrain where the coefficient of friction between tyre and ground is low. This chapter sets out to discuss and to lay down techniques to deal with these topics.

Equivalent Mass (M_E)

When a vehicle is accelerating, the resultant propulsive force on the

44

vehicle, that is the tractive force at the drive wheels less the vehicle drag force, accelerates the mass of the vehicle, the inertia of the road wheels, the engine and the transmission. It is convenient, when performing vehicle performance calculations, to express these terms together in what is termed the "equivalent mass" (M_E) of the vehicle. This may be formulated as follows:

$$\text{The force on the vehicle, } F = (T - T_e) \times \eta_T \times \frac{g_a \times g_g}{r_r} \qquad 4.1$$

where T = the steady-state torque delivered by the engine

$\quad \eta_T$ = the overall efficiency of the transmission system, as discussed below

$\quad g_a$ = the drive axle ratio (input speed/output speed)

$\quad g_g$ = the gearbox ratio (input speed/output speed)

$\quad r_r$ = the rolling radius of the drive wheels

$\quad T_e$ = the inertia torque of the engine = $\dfrac{I_e \times g_a \times g_g \times f}{r_r}$

where f = the vehicle acceleration.

Thus, the force on the vehicle,

$$F = F_T - \left(I_e \times \eta_T \times \left(\frac{g_a \times g_g}{r_r} \right)^2 \times f \right) \qquad 4.2$$

where the tractive force,

$$F_T = T \times \eta_T \times \frac{g_a \times g_g}{r_r} \qquad 4.3$$

Now the force (F) on the vehicle is required to accelerate the mass (M_v) of the vehicle, the inertia of the road wheels (I_w), the inertia of the transmission, or propeller shaft (I_p) and to overcome the drag force (Fd).

We have then, from Newton's second law, that

$$F_T - \left[I_e \times \eta_T \times \left(\frac{g_a \times g_g}{r_r} \right)^2 \times f \right] - F_d = \left[M_V + \frac{I_w}{r_r^2} + \left(I_p \times \left(\frac{g_a}{r_r} \right)^2 \right) \right] f$$

From which the propulsive force on the vehicle is given by

$$F_p = F_T - F_d = f \left[M_V + \frac{I_w}{r_r^2} + \left(I_p \times \left(\frac{g_a}{r_r} \right)^2 \right) + \left(I_e \times \eta_T \times \left(\frac{g_a \times g_g}{r_r} \right)^2 \right) \right] \quad 4.4$$

This may be compared to

$$F_p = f.m_E$$

obtained by applying Newton's second law to an accelerating vehicle of equivalent mass (M_E) yielding

$$M_E = M_V + \frac{I_w}{r_r^2} + \left(I_p \times \left(\frac{g_g}{r_r} \right)^2 \right) + \left(I_e \times \eta_T \times \left(\frac{g_a \times g_g}{r_2} \right)^2 \right) \quad 4.5$$

Note that the equivalent inertia of the engine contains the transmission efficiency (η_T) term. Ideally, component parts of this global term should appear elsewhere in expression 4.5 but, surprisingly, so little is known of the formulation of transmission efficiency that it is usually expressed as the single, combined term.

Transmission Efficiency (η_T)

Little is known of the formulation of transmission efficiency because it has not been easy to measure. For a conventional manual transmission it is known to be high, usually around the 90% mark, but to assess it by the measurement of torque levels invariably results in a band of scatter stretching from 70% to 110%. Clearly an unsatisfactory procedure when one wishes to obtain the variation of transmission efficiency with important independent variables.

The term describes that proportion of the power lost in friction, viscous and windage effects between the flywheel of the engine and the tyres of the drive wheels. It does not include inertial power of an accelerating drive-line, nor does it include the tyre distortion effects. It is therefore, the mechanical efficiency of the drive train which, for a conventional transmission, is the gearbox, complete with bearings and gears, the prop. shaft with its bearings, the drive axle with its bearings and gears and the drive wheel bearings.

For work on the calculation of the time-to-speed of a vehicle the transmission efficiency of a unit should be expressed as a function of the input torque, the input speed, the gear ratio and the oil viscosity. Rarely, however, does data for such a function exist. To express the transmission efficiency by a single number, say 0.90, is not enough for time-to-speed calculations. Therefore, in the absence of anything better, it is recommended that the following expression be used.

$$\eta_T = [0.96 - 0.000707.V - 0.000029.V^2] \times \\ [0.998(1 - 0.007(NG - I)) - 0.0001965(2.08^{NG-I}.V)] \qquad 4.6$$

where V = vehicle speed m/s
     NG = No. of gear ratios
       I = the particular gear number

The first term in square brackets (the quadratic) describes a typical drive axle efficiency. The remaining term describes the efficiency of a typical gearbox; the efficiency and the slope of the efficiency versus speed curve decreasing slightly with the lower gear ratios.

Gradient

Fig. 4.1 depicts the forces acting upon a vehicle when moving at a steady speed upon a gradient. For the purpose of this work we shall avoid the often used descriptor of a gradient as being a slope of 1 in N, largely because a level road must then be described as being 1 in infinity and, if a computer is to be used in any subsequent calculation work, the term infinity would be an embarrassment. A secondary reason for the avoidance of this descriptor is that some authorities say that it denotes a rise of 1 metre in height for every N metres travelled along the slope while others say that it represents a rise of 1 metre in height for every N metres along the horizontal plane. In the former definition therefore 1/N gives the sine of the angle θ while in the latter $1/N$ gives the tangent of θ. Unless clearly defined therefore, an ambiguity could arise.

The descriptor used in this work is

$$i = Sin\theta \qquad\qquad 4.7$$

Thus the downhill component of the vehicle weight is W.i and, since this is in the opposite direction to the direction of motion, it may be included in the drag expression to give

$$F_d = M_v.g. \, (Ad+i+Bd.V) + C_d. \, \tfrac{1}{2}\rho A.(V+V_w)^2 \qquad\qquad 4.8$$

This should be compared with expression 1.9 in chapter 1. It is convenient therefore that the gradient may be accommodated by a simple extension of the drag expression. Should, however, the vehicle be travelling downhill instead of uphill, the term (i) in the drag expression becomes negative.

For a level road $i = 0$, and for a vertical cliff face such that $\theta = 90°$; $i = 1$. This way of describing a gradient is often used in a slightly modified form and termed the "percentage grade"; this being i x 100. Thus one talks of a 20% grade; i being 0.2.

This description of a gradient is related to the description 1 in N (N being measured along the slope) by $i = 1/N$.

Position of the Centre of Gravity

This position may be defined as shown in Fig. 4.1 as the distance (a) aft of the front wheel centre line, the distance (b) in front of the rear wheel centre line and the height (h) above the ground plane. These dimensions may be obtained from the vehicle manufacturer or measured by the following procedure.

Chock the suspension of the vehicle solid and inflate the tyres to some 400 kN/m² ($\approx$60 lbf/in²) pressure. Measure the rolling radius (r_r) of the wheels and arrange hitch brackets at the front and at the rear of the vehicle in the plane of the wheel centres, Fig. 4.2. Raise the front and then the rear of the vehicle successively in small increments through the medium of a load cell to produce data

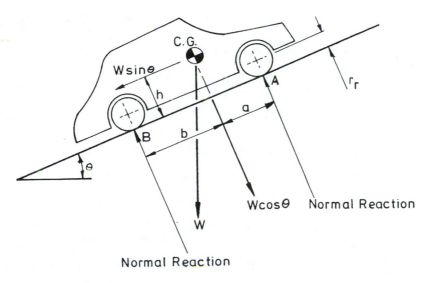

FIGURE 4.1

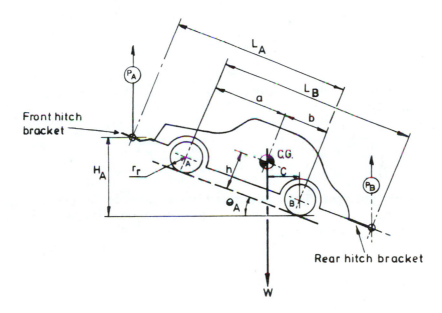

FIGURE 4.2   Measurement of the position of the centre of gravity

relating the load cell reading (P) to the angle of inclination of the vehicle (θ).

Taking moments about A in Fig. 4.2, when the front end is raised, shows this relationship to be

$$P_A = \frac{W}{L_A} [b - (h-r_r) \, \text{Tan} \, \theta_A] \qquad\qquad 4.9$$

where L_A is the distance between the rear wheel centre line and the front hitch point and

$$\theta_A = \text{Sin}^{-1} \frac{(H_A - y_f)}{L_A} \qquad\qquad 4.10$$

where y_f is the height of the front hitch point when the vehicle is level.

Similarly, when the rear end is raised taking moments about B affords

$$P_B = \frac{W}{L_B} [a - (h-r_r) \, \text{Tan} \, \theta_B] \qquad\qquad 4.11$$

Where L_B is the distance between the front wheel centre-line and the rear hitch point and

$$\theta_B = \text{Sin}^{-1} \left(\frac{H_B - y_r}{L_B} \right) \qquad\qquad 4.12$$

Where y_r is the height of the rear hitch point when the vehicle is level and W is the weight of the vehicle, including the hitch brackets.

Plotting a graph therefore of load cell reading P_A against Tan θ_A should yield a straight line, the slope equalling $-W/L_A (h-r_r)$ and the intercept $W.b/L_A$. From these h and b (and hence a) may be determined. These values may be checked by using the load cell (P_B) versus Tanθ_B data from raising the rear end of the vehicle. The purpose of collecting data from a number of values of vehicle inclination (θ) and the plotting of graphs, rather than the use of one value only of θ, is to enable experimental error to be minimised by the drawing of a straight line through the experimental points.

Overturning on a Gradient

If the torque delivered to the axle of a rear wheel drive vehicle is too high the vehicle may overturn in pitch; that is that the front wheels may be raised from the ground. This is a rare occurrence in conventional motor cars but it is an all too frequent accident with agricultural tractors and may occur with a motor cycle. It is important therefore that the vehicle designer should be aware of any such possibility and a system of vehicle performance calculations should include a check.

Taking the general case of a vehicle on a gradient, Fig. 4.1, and the worst condition of the maximum engine torque in conjunction with the engagement of first gear results in the condition that

$$T_{max} \times g_a \times g_{g(1st)} < W(b.Cos\theta - (h-r_r)Sin\theta) \qquad 4.13$$

should be true to avoid overturning in pitch.

Vehicle "take off" from Rest

In calculating the time-to-speed from rest of a vehicle having a conventional manual transmission, a difficulty arises in dealing with clutch slip. Immediately before "take-off", the vehicle speed is zero and the engine speed is relatively high. A few seconds after t = 0 the engine speed is directly related to vehicle speed and the clutch slip speed is zero. During these few seconds the vehicle has accelerated and the engine may have decelerated, that is to say, the clutch has slipped. A technique must be devised therefore to deal with the torque transmission down the drive-line during this period.

The system may be modelled in the manner depicted in Fig.4.3. This shows, on the left hand side of the clutch, the engine subsystem of inertia (I_e), engine torque (T_e) which, in general, is a function of engine speed (ω_e) and throttle angle ($\emptyset$) and an opposing clutch slip

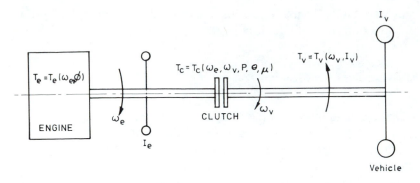

FIGURE 4.3   Model of clutch engagement

torque (T_c). This latter torque is a function of the force (P) pressing the clutch plates together (sometimes termed the clamp load) and the coefficient of friction (μ) between the working surfaces. This may be expressed as

$$T_c = P.\mu \left(\frac{r_1 + r_2}{2} \right) \times N° \text{ of active faces} \qquad 4.14$$

where r_1 and r_2 are the inner and outer radii respectively of the clutch.

The coefficient of friction (μ) however, is not of constant value during a clutch engagement although it simplifies matters considerably if it may be considered to be so. In general, it is a function of slip speed ($\omega_e - \omega_v$) and temperature, both of which alter in value considerably during an engagement.

The subsystem on the right hand side of Fig. 4.3 represents the vehicle driven through its drive-line. The mass of the vehicle and the inertia of the wheels are expressed as an equivalent inertia on the output from clutch shaft in an analogous manner to that outlined earlier in this chapter.

The drag force (F_d) on the vehicle may be expressed as an equivalent torque in the output from clutch shaft,

$$T_v = \frac{F_d \times r_r}{g_a \times g_g} \qquad 4.15$$

and this is a function of vehicle speed (V) or clutch output shaft speed (ω_v) because the drag force is a function of V. Driving this subsystem is the clutch torque T_c given by expression 4.14.

This model enables two equations of motion describing the two subsystems to be set up. They are

$$\frac{d\omega_e}{dt} = \frac{T_e - T_c}{I_e} \qquad\qquad 4.16$$

and

$$\frac{d\omega_v}{dt} = \frac{T_c - T_v}{I_v} \qquad\qquad 4.17$$

Since T_c is a function of clamp load (P) and temperature (θ), equations expressing these two parameters must be set up. The first may be obtained by noting the manner in which a driver operates a clutch. This is to say that we write

$$\frac{dp}{dt} = \text{some specified function} \qquad\qquad 4.18$$

in conjunction with some function to describe the manipulation of the engine throttle.

The second may be dealt with by the setting up of the partial differential equation governing one-dimensional heat conduction through the clutch, viz

$$\frac{\delta\theta}{\delta t} = \alpha . \frac{\delta^2\theta}{\delta x^2} \qquad\qquad 4.19$$

where α = the thermal diffusivity and x is the distance into the material of the clutch from some datum plane. In conjunction with 4.14, the rate of heat generation at the working face may be expressed as

$$\frac{dQ}{dt} = T_c \, (\omega_e - \omega_v) \qquad\qquad 4.20$$

and the manner in which the coefficient of friction varies with temperature and slip speed must be known.

These ordinary differential equations and the one partial differential equation may be solved using suitable numerical techniques; clearly a formidable task considering the short time involved compared with the total time of a time-to-speed test. This set of equations, including the manner in which a driver operates a clutch (expression 4.18), has been investigated thoroughly at Loughborough. The resulting computer program is large. Even so, it was found that, for a reasonable representation of the heat transfer pattern, the two dimensional form of expression 4.19 was necessary.

It is apparent that some short cut must be found to deal with vehicle take-off. It is possible to assume that the coefficient of friction remains constant, a typical value being $\mu = 0.3$ This avoids the necessity of the partial differential equation governing the heat transfer. The manner in which a driver operates a clutch (expression 4.18) may be expressed as a simple step function for a time-to-speed calculation on the grounds that, for repeatability of experimental results, a test driver may be instructed to apply the full clamp load in zero time at the instant $t = 0$. This technique eliminates the driver element from the results of the test. However, for normal driving, a simple step function is not adequate; a driver deliberately slips his clutch. This is particularly in evidence when a vehicle is being started from rest on a steep gradient.

However, while these assumptions simplify considerably the calculation procedure, it is still rather involved for a small part of the overall time-to-speed calculation. For the vast majority of time-to-speed calculations, the simple technique outlined below has been found to be satisfactory.

A clutch is designed, usually, to transmit torque some 20% greater than maximum engine torque only. A greater capacity may result in a "harsh" clutch. If we work on the assumption that the driver's instructions are to depress both the clutch and throttle pedals immediately prior to the test and at the instant $t = 0$ to slide his foot off the clutch pedal, any influence from the driver is eliminated. Some torque benefit may be gained from the decelerating engine by following this procedure, but the net torque transmitted through the clutch cannot exceed its capacity. A very simple approximation therefore is to assume that the maximum engine torque is transmitted during the clutch slip period.

This technique may seem to be crude but by following the above procedure at the start of a time-to-speed test a high torque level may be transmitted which, at times, may exceed the maximum steady state torque output of the engine. Also, the time involved during the clutch slip period is small compared with the time for a vehicle to complete a time-to-speed run. In view of the immense simplification in the calculation procedure therefore it is reasonable to assume maximum engine torque during the take-off of the vehicle.

Wheel-spin

This term is used to describe that characteristic lack of adhesion between tyre and road normally associated with high performance cars starting from rest or more mundane vehicles on a slippery road. If too much torque is supplied to the drive wheels than can be maintained by the friction between tyre and road, slippage or wheel-spin will result. The possibility of such an occurrence must therefore be a feature of any performance calculation procedure.

Wholesale slippage between tyre and road introduces problems in calculating the time-to-speed of a vehicle. Will the driver maintain full throttle and brazen out the wheel-spin period, or will he reduce the throttle opening in order to stop the wheel-spin? If he adopts the former there is no longer any straightforward relationship between engine speed and vehicle speed. Further, the coefficient of friction between tyre and road diminishes as the slip speed increases. As this slip speed is not known, the engine speed and thus the tractive force are not known and a great deal has to be known about the character of the coefficient of friction to enable them to be calculated.

If the latter technique is adopted the question of driver response arises. How long will it take the driver to realise that wheel-spin is occurring and to what extent will he reduce his throttle setting?

The matter may be resolved if it is assumed that a professional driver is at the wheel and that he is capable of adjusting his throttle

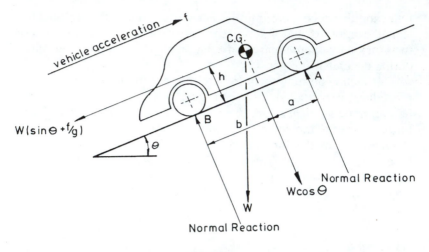

FIGURE 4.4

setting instantaneously to maintain the vehicle on the point of wheel-spin during the wheel spin period. Using this assumption there is no slippage between tyre and road, thus the static coefficient of friction applies and the normal relationship between vehicle speed and engine speed fixed by the gearing exists. Also, there is no driver response time to take into consideration. A good driver, familiar with his test vehicle, is capable of achieving very nearly the ideal implicit in this assumption. Certainly it simplifies the calculation procedures considerably.

Fig. 4.4 depicts the general case of an accelerating vehicle upon a gradient. The product (coefficient of friction × normal reaction between road and drive wheels), termed "the limiting tractive force", is given by

$$F_l = \frac{\mu . M_v . g}{(a+b)} \left\{ a . \sqrt{1-i^2} + h \left(i + \frac{f}{g} \right) \right\} \qquad 4.21$$

for a rear wheel drive vehicle and by

$$F_l = \frac{\mu . M_v . g}{(a+b)} \left\{ b . \sqrt{1-i^2} - h \left(i + \frac{f}{g} \right) \right\} \qquad 4.22$$

for a front wheel drive vehicle. The vehicle acceleration is denoted by (f) and the acceleration due to gravity by (g).

This limiting tractive force therefore determines the maximum possible acceleration of the vehicle. Any drive force greater than this will result in wheel-spin. The drive force accelerates the vehicle mass and that of the free road wheels, opposes the aerodynamic drag and the gradient term in the drag equation (4.8) and finally caters for the rolling resistance of the free road wheels.

Thus, for a conventional type of vehicle having half its road wheels as drive wheels the drive force is

$$F = f \left[M_v + \frac{I_w}{2r_r^2} \right] + \text{Aero. drag} + M_v.g.i.$$

$$+ \frac{M_v.g}{(a+b)} \times \left(b \sqrt{1-i^2} - h(i + \frac{f}{g}) (Ad+Bd.V) \right) \qquad 4.23$$

Equating this to the limiting tractive force and using the drag force expression (4.8) produces an expression for the greatest possible vehicle acceleration. In the case of a rear wheel drive vehicle, this is

$$f_{max} = \frac{\frac{\mu M_v.g}{(a+b)} \left\{ (a \sqrt{1-i^2} + h.i) (\mu+Ad+Bd.V) - Fd \right\}}{M_v + \frac{I_w}{2.r_r^2} - \frac{M_v.h}{(a+b)} (\mu+Ad+Bd.V)} \qquad 4.24$$

and in the case of a front wheel drive vehicle, we have

$$f_{max} = \frac{\frac{\mu M_v.g}{(a+b)} \left\{ (b \sqrt{1-i^2} - h.i) (\mu+Ad+Bd.V) - Fd \right\}}{M_v + \frac{I_w}{2.r_r^2} + \frac{M_v.h}{(a+b)} (\mu+Ad+Bd.V)} \qquad 4.25$$

where the vehicle drag, Fd, includes the rolling resistance, the aerodynamic drag and the gradient.

These show that the front wheel drive vehicle is more susceptible to wheel spin when compared with a similar rear wheel drive vehicle having the same centre of gravity position.

In the case of a vehicle driven on all four wheels the limiting tractive force is

$$F_l = \mu.M_v.g. \sqrt{1 - i^2} \qquad\qquad 4.26$$

which is opposed by the inertia force, the aerodynamic drag and the gradient term in the drag expression. Thus the drive force is

$$F = f.M_v + \tfrac{1}{2}.\rho.A.C._d (V+V_w)^2 + W.i$$

giving the greatest possible vehicle acceleration as

$$f_{max} = g \left\{ (\mu \sqrt{1-i^2} - i) - \frac{\rho.A.Cd}{2.Mv.g} (V+V_w)^2 \right\} \qquad 4.27$$

Throughout a time-to-speed calculation therefore it is necessary to check that the application of Newton's second law to the accelerating vehicle does not result in an acceleration greater than the appropriate expression for the greatest possible vehicle acceleration (4.24, 4.25 or 4.27). If it does, then "wheel-spin" will result and the calculations may be continued by resetting the value of vehicle acceleration to this greatest possible value.

Tyre Growth

The final consideration is that the rolling radius of the wheels may change with vehicle speed. An investigation has shown this to be of little importance in vehicle performance calculations but its effect should, nevertheless, be included. The so-called "Dunlop" Formula expresses this as a function of V^2, which seems to be logical since the centrifugal stress in a rotating body such as a tyre, varies with V^2. Thus

$$r_{r_v} = r_r \times \left[1 + K.V^2\right] \qquad\qquad 4.28$$

where r_{r_v} = the rolling radius at vehicle speed V

r_r = the rolling radius at zero speed

and K is the tyre growth factor; being zero for a radial ply tyre and equal to 23.83×10^{-6} for a cross ply tyre when the vehicle speed (V) is expressed in m/s units (1.84×10^{-6} when V is in km/h units and 4.76×10^{-6} when V is in mile/h units).

5 Time-to-Speed and Maximum Speed Calculations (Manual Transmission)

This chapter is concerned with the full power performance of vehicles having "manual" transmissions. That of automatic transmission vehicles is better treated separately and is described in Chapter 10.

The time for a vehicle to accelerate between speeds V_1 and V_2 is afforded by effecting the integral

$$t = \int_{V_1}^{V_2} \frac{1}{f} \, dV \qquad\qquad 5.1$$

Although expression 5.1. is simple, stemming directly from the definition of acceleration $f = {}^{dV}/_{dt}$, it is difficult to integrate it analytically because the acceleration (f) is an awkward function of speed (V). It is best performed therefore using some numerical technique. That is to say that the independent variable V is taken progressively from the lower limit of speed V_1 in small steps, the acceleration being evaluated at each step, until the upper value of V_2 is reached.

This is represented in Fig. 5.1., being a plot of $^1/_f$ against V. The discontinuities in slope are the gear change points. The area under the curve between V_1 and V_2 therefore is the time to accelerate between these limits. The speed range is shown divided into a number of small increments, each one of which may be considered to be trapezoidal in shape such that its area is

$$\Delta \text{ area} = \Delta t = \left[\frac{1/_{fa} + 1/_{fb}}{2} \right] \Delta V \qquad\qquad 5.2$$

60

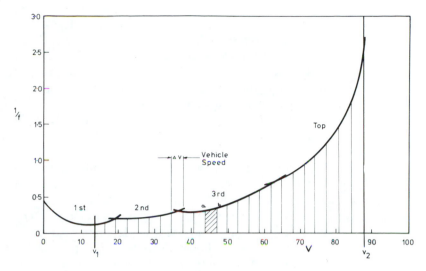

FIGURE 5.1   Time to speed calculation

suffices (a) and (b) denoting the beginning and end of a step length.

The procedure therefore is to evaluate the reciprocal of the acceleration at the beginning of every step length, starting at V_1 and progressing to V_2, and to sum continually the area in the manner described by expression 5.2. It may be noted that the shape of the curve in Fig. 5.1 is always concave upwards thus incurring an accumulative error in the summing process. This may be reduced to negligible proportions by selecting a large number of steps; 25 to 50 being found to be adequate for most practical purposes. A good check on this error is to evaluate the time-to-speed for a particular vehicle using, say, 25 steps in the numerical integration and then to repeat the process using 50 steps and to note the difference.

In a similar manner, the distance travelled (s) by the vehicle may be calculated since

$$\Delta s = (V_a + \frac{\Delta V}{2}) \Delta t \qquad\qquad 5.3$$

Δt being the time taken to cover the speed increment ΔV and the term inside the bracket being the average speed of the increment.

It is now apposite to consider the gear change speeds. Clearly, it is illogical to consider these as independent variables; numbers which are determined before the calculation procedure begins. While past experience may well give a very good indication of when a gear change should be made in the case of a conventional vehicle specification, it is manifestly an unsatisfactory procedure for the unconventional specification. Here it must be remembered that one of the main uses of a time-to-speed calculation procedure is in studying the effect of a particular design parameter, say the axle ratio. In such a parametric study the axle ratio or any other design parameter may be altered from a very low to a very high value in order that its effect on the time-to-speed may be studied. It is doubtful if satisfactory gear change speeds could be pre-specified for all such calculations. The logical procedure therefore is to treat these as dependent variables and to devise a criterion by which they may be determined.

One obvious criterion is that a gear change shall be made when it is found that the vehicle acceleration would be greater in another gear to that which is currently engaged. At each vehicle speed step therefore, the vehicle acceleration is evaluated for each of the gear ratios and that which gives the greatest acceleration is selected as being the gear ratio currently being used. If this is found to be different from that used during the previous speed step, a gear change may be said to have been made. This procedure has been found to work very well in practice and to predict satisfactorily the gear change speeds used by a professional driver when testing a vehicle.

The time-to-speed calculation procedure should start by specifying the relevant engine, transmission, vehicle and environmental data. These are

1) engine

    1.1. torque curve

    1.2. minimum speed

    1.3. maximum speed

    1.4. inertia (I_e)

2) transmission

    2.1. gear ratios (g_g)

    2.2. drive axle ratio (g_a)

2.3. rolling radius (r_r) at zero speed.

2.4. propeller shaft inertia (I_p)

2.5. total road wheel inertia (I_w)

2.6. tyre growth factor (K)

2.7. whether a front, or rear wheel or a four wheel drive vehicle

2.8. gear change time

3) vehicle

3.1. Mass (M_v)

3.2. position of the centre of gravity (a, b and h)

3.3. drag coefficients (A_d, B_d and C_d)

3.4. projected frontal area (A)

4) environmental

4.1. initial speed (V_1) (usually zero)

4.2. final speed (V_2)

4.3. coefficient or friction (μ)

4.4. gradient (i)

4.5. wind speed (V_w)

For each incremental vehicle speed V, the acceleration of the vehicle in each of the gears may be determined using the following calculation procedure

(a) dynamic rolling radius, r_{r_v} (expression 4.28)

(b) drag force, F_d (expression 4.8)

(c) overall gear ratio,

$$G = \frac{2\pi}{60} \times \frac{r_{r_v}}{g_g \cdot g_a} \text{ m/s per rev/min of engine speed} \qquad 5.4$$

(d) engine speed, $N_e = V/G$ rev/min

(e) check to see if the engine speed so determined is within the allowable engine speed range. If it is not, it is not permissible to use this particular gear ratio.

(f) transmission efficiency, η_T, from expression 4.6 or from experimental data.

(g) tractive force, $F_t = T_e \times \dfrac{g_g \times g_a}{r_{r_v}} \times \eta_T$ 5.5

(h) propulsive force $F_p = F_t - F_d$ 5.6.

(i) equivalent mass of the vehicle, M_E (expression 4.5)

(j) vehicle acceleration $f = F_p/M_E$ 5.7.

Having obtained the vehicle acceleration in the particular gear, a check should be made for wheel-spin by comparing this value with the greatest possible acceleration given by expression 4.24, 4.25 or 4.27. If greater than f_{max}, the effect is wheel-spin and the acceleration value must be reset.

Next the gear affording the greatest vehicle acceleration is designated as being the current gear and the incremental time evaluated using expression 5.2. This incremental time must include also the gear change time if the gear ratio of the current step is different from that of the previous step.

The incremental distance travelled may then be evaluated using expression 5.3 and the cumulative time and distance evaluated by adding the increments to the previous totals. This calculation procedure lends itself very readily to the use of a digital computer and the output may be arranged on the lines of Table 5.1, being a time-to-speed calculation on a small motor car the specification of which is given in Table 5.2.

Maximum vehicle speed is again a full throttle condition, defined by the cross-over point between the engine full throttle power line and the load line. Fig. 5.2 shows these two lines arranged to cross to the right of the maximum power speed (Np) of the engine by the suitable choice of axle ratio. This represents the "undergeared" condition and provides more power for acceleration, the vertical difference between the two lines, than the converse, or "overgeared", case. In the latter, the load line is arranged to cross the engine power line to the left of the maximum power point. This results in better economy, because the load line is closer to the optimum control line, and a quieter engine because its speed is lower.

The neutral condition, neither undergeared or overgeared, is afforded when the load line crosses the full power line at the maximum engine power point. This provides the greatest possible

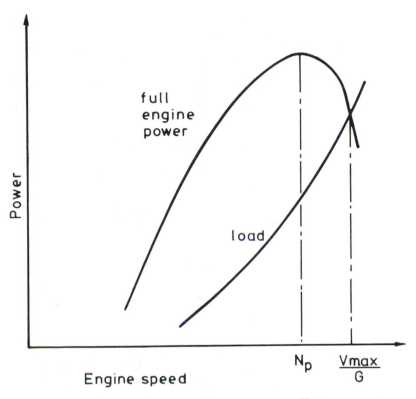

Power

Engine speed

$$N_p \qquad \frac{Vmax}{G}$$

FIGURE 5.2   Degree of undergearing, $\lambda = \dfrac{V_{max}}{Np.G}$

maximum vehicle speed. If the cross-over point is to the right or to the left, the maximum vehicle speed drops slightly.

The "degree of undergearing" therefore is a matter of compromise and is in the control of the designer since it is fixed by the overall top gear ratio. Turning again to Fig. 5.2 it may be seen that the engine speed at the cross-over point is given by

$$N_{V_{max}} = \frac{V_{max}}{G} \qquad\qquad 5.8$$

where the overall gear ratio (G) is as defined by expression 5.4. Thus, the degree of undergearing may be conveniently defined as

TABLE 5.1
RESULT OF TIME-TO-SPEED CALCULATION

Vehicle Speed			Accln. m/s/s	Drag N	Gear No.	Time s	Distance m	Tract & Force	Prop N	Eng.Speed rev/min
mile/h	km/h	m/s								
Gear Change to Ratio 1 Gear Change Speed (mile/h) = 20.00										
0.00	0.00	0.00	1.997	176.52	1	0.000	0.00	3651.56	3475.04	2575.0
2.00	3.22	0.89	1.997	176.93	1	0.448	0.20	3645.08	3468.15	2575.0
4.00	6.44	1.79	1.990	178.16	1	0.897	0.80	3638.28	3460.11	2545.0
6.00	9.66	2.68	1.985	180.22	1	1.347	1.81	3631.15	3450.93	2515.0
8.00	12.87	3.58	1.980	183.10	1	1.798	3.22	3623.69	3440.59	2515.0
10.00	16.09	4.47	1.974	186.80	1	2.250	5.04	3613.76	3426.96	2680.3
12.00	19.31	5.36	1.919	191.33	1	2.710	7.30	3520.82	3329.49	3119.7
14.00	22.53	6.26	1.820	196.68	1	3.188	10.08	3352.14	3155.46	3638.7
16.00	25.75	7.15	1.703	202.85	1	3.697	13.49	3153.37	2950.52	4157.4
18.00	28.97	8.05	1.571	209.85	1	4.244	17.65	2930.39	2720.55	4675.5
Gear Change to Ratio 2 Gear Change Speed (mile/h) = 20.00										
20.00	32.18	8.94	1.454	217.66	2	4.836	22.67	2063.39	1845.73	3039.9
22.00	35.40	9.83	1.406	226.31	2	5.461	28.54	2010.70	1784.40	3342.5
24.00	38.62	10.73	1.360	235.77	2	6.110	35.22	1948.01	1712.24	3644.8
26.00	41.84	11.62	1.289	246.06	2	6.788	42.80	1879.95	1633.90	3946.6
28.00	45.06	12.52	1.224	257.17	2	7.500	51.39	1808.51	1551.34	4248.0
30.00	48.28	13.41	1.155	269.10	2	8.252	61.14	1732.26	1463.16	4549.0
32.00	51.49	14.30	1.077	281.86	2	9.054	72.25	1645.59	1363.73	4849.4
34.00	54.71	15.20	0.982	295.43	2	9.924	85.09	1537.75	1242.32	5149.2
36.00	57.93	16.09	0.856	309.84	2	10.902	100.39	1391.92	1082.08	5448.5

Gear Change to Ratio 3 Gear Change Speed (mile/h) = 38.00

38.00	61.15	16.99	0.753	325.06	3	12.018	118.85	1160.07	835.01	3352.5
40.00	64.37	17.88	0.719	341.11	3	13.234	140.04	1138.08	796.97	3326.3
42.00	67.59	18.77	0.683	357.98	3	14.510	163.44	1114.82	756.84	3699.8
44.00	70.80	19.67	0.645	375.67	3	15.858	189.34	1090.72	715.05	3872.8
46.00	74.02	20.56	0.606	394.19	3	17.288	218.11	1066.02	671.83	4045.4
48.00	77.24	21.46	0.566	413.53	3	18.814	250.18	1040.77	627.24	4217.5
50.00	80.46	22.35	0.525	433.69	3	20.455	286.13	1014.78	581.08	4389.2
52.00	83.68	23.24	0.481	454.68	3	22.236	326.72	987.64	532.96	4560.3
54.00	86.90	24.14	0.436	476.49	3	24.190	373.03	958.66	482.17	4731.0
54.00	86.90	24.14	0.436	476.49	3	24.190	373.03	958.66	482.17	4731.0

Quarter Mile Mark Passed Speed = 55.09 mile/hour, Time = 25.4 Seconds approx.

56.00	90.12	25.03	0.387	499.12	3	26.373	426.69	926.86	427.74	4901.1
58.00	93.33	25.93	0.333	522.57	3	28.871	490.35	890.96	368.39	5070.8
60.00	96.55	26.82	0.274	546.85	3	31.847	568.84	849.34	302.49	5239.8
62.00	99.77	27.71	0.206	571.95	3	35.647	672.47	800.03	228.08	5408.2

Gear Change to Ratio 4 Gear Change Speed (mile/h) = 64.00

64.00	102.99	28.61	0.145	597.88	4	40.891	820.17	752.96	155.08	3982.9
66.00	106.21	29.50	0.108	624.62	4	48.118	1030.17	739.65	115.03	4102.4
68.00	109.43	30.40	0.069	652.19	4	58.716	1347.59	726.18	73.99	4221.4

Time to Speed on Stated Gradient (Secs) = 58.72

TABLE 5.2
DETAILS OF SMALL MOTOR CAR

1.1   Torque polynomial (6th order) coefficients

$$T_e = 0.252 + 64.94 \left(\frac{N_e}{1000}\right) - 23.23 \left(\frac{N_e}{1000}\right)^2 + 3.900 \left(\frac{N_e}{1000}\right)^3 - 0.570 \left(\frac{N_e}{1000}\right)^4$$

$$+ 0.094 \left(\frac{N_e}{1000}\right)^5 - 0.0077 \left(\frac{N_e}{1000}\right)^6$$

(units of engine torque T_e are (Nm) and engine speed N_e (rev/min))
1.2   minimum engine speed, 1000 rev/min
1.3   maximum engine speed, 6300 rev/min
1.4   engine inertia, $I_e = 0.20$ kg m^2
2.1   gear ratios are 4.10, 2.40, 1.40 and 1.00
2.2   axle ratio, $g_a = 4.44$
2.3   rolling radius of wheels, $r_r = 0.30$ m
2.4   propeller shaft inertia, negligible
2.5   total road wheel inertia, $I_w = 2.70$ kg m^2
2.6   rear wheel drive
2.8   gear change time, zero
3.1   vehicle mass, $M_v = 1000$ kg
3.2   position of the centre of gravity, a = 1.13 m, b = 1.17 m, h = 0.50 m
3.3   drag coefficients, Ad = 0.018, Bd = 0, Cd = 0.45
3.4   projected frontal area, A = 1.86 m^2
4.1   initial speed $V_1 = 0$
4.2   final speed $V_2 = 68$ mile/h (30.4 m/s or 109.4 km/h)
4.3   coefficient of friction between tyre and road, $\mu = 1$
4.4   gradient, i = 0

The degree of undergearing, $\lambda = \dfrac{V_{max}}{N_p \times G}$ 5.9

This makes $\lambda > 1$ for the undergeared case; $\lambda < 1$ for the overgeared and $\lambda = 1$ for the neutral case. 10% undergearing therefore is provided by making $\lambda = 1.1$ and 10% overgearing by arranging that $\lambda = 0.9$.

At maximum vehicle speed on the level road, under zero wind conditions, the power required by the vehicle at the engine flywheel (brake power) is given by

$$P_v = \frac{F_d \times V_{max}}{\eta_T}$$

$$= \left[M_v.g.(Ad + Bd.V_{max}) + \tfrac{1}{2}\rho.A.Cd.V_{max}^2 \right] \frac{V_{max}}{\eta T} \qquad 5.10$$

and the power supplied by the engine is

$$P_e = T_e(N_p \times \lambda) \times N_p \times \lambda \times \frac{2\pi}{60} \qquad 5.11$$

where T_e (Nm) is the engine torque and N_p (rev/min) is the engine speed of maximum power. Equating the expressions for P_v and P_e and solving for V_{max} yields the cubic in V_{max} and because the transmission efficiency (η_T) should be a function of speed, it is recommended that an iterative method of solution be used. That is to guess the maximum speed, evaluate the overall gear ratio and so determine the corresponding engine speed and torque output and the degree of undergearing, calculate the vehicle drag and the transmission efficiency and then see if $P_v = P_e$. If not, try another value of V_{max}. Use of the data in Table 5.2. will show top gear maximum speed of this small motor car to be 71.3 mile/h (114.7 km/h or 31.9 m/s); using expression 4.6 for the transmission efficiency η_T.

6 Fuel Consumption Calculation and the Effect of some Design Parameters

An interest in the rate at which fuel is consumed by a vehicle is essentially an interest in part load operation. The fuel consumption of a vehicle subject to a time-to-speed test may be of passing interest, but cannot be of paramount importance since the object of the test is to attain a high speed as rapidly as possible. The single, full power curve used to describe the engine in Chapter 5 therefore is scarcely relevant. Data on the engine power output at all other load conditions, or throttle positions, in the manner described in Chapter 3 and characterised by Fig. 3.5, is required.

In order to calculate the expected fuel consumption of a vehicle at the design stage it is necessary to specify the operation of the vehicle. It is understandable that the vehicle manufacturer may wish to define this operation by detailing a typical type of journey in order that he may calculate the overall fuel consumption of his vehicle. But this will change markedly with the duty of the vehicle. The second car of a two-car family may be used almost entirely for very short journeys of the order of 1 or 2 km in length whereas an identical car owned by a neighbour may be subject to predominately motorway travel. This wide range of usage is true also of the smaller type of commercial vehicle. While a typical route may not be an adequate description for all types of duty of a vehicle it may be satisfactory for one particular class, say, predominately motorway travel or, perhaps, urban travel.

However, the operation of a vehicle under transient conditions introduces problems in the calculation of fuel consumption. Consider for a moment the use of the choke when starting from cold on a winter's day. This is known to increase the fuel consumption dramatically, but how much choke is necessary, and for how long? The answer to these questions depends upon the temperature and humidity of the day as well as the number of road junctions and density of traffic encountered during the first 5 km of the journey. Indeed, it depends upon the driver also, since some, rather than use the choke, will operate the accelerator pump to prevent the engine from dying after the vehicle has negotiated a hazard such as a road junction.

All this, as well as every junction, bend, gradient and gear change must be specified. Further, since the driver has a marked effect on fuel consumption when operating the vehicle under transient conditions, the type of driver should be detailed; a formidable task. There have been a number of attempts to calculate fuel consumption in this manner but the problems detailed above and lack of knowledge of the engine behaviour under transient operation makes the result unsatisfactory in view of the amount of calculation involved.

A more satisfactory technique is to calculate the steady-state fuel consumption at different speeds throughout the speed range of the vehicle. This is detailed below and is a straight-forward procedure. It is independent of the transient operation of the engine and the caprices of the driver. Further, the steady-state fuel consumption of the vehicle is easy to measure and may yield information of a more fundamental nature on the match between a particular engine, transmission and vehicle. Our aim should be therefore to relate transient conditions to the steady-state operation, rather than attempt to deal with the transient operation direct.

The study of the match between engine, transmission and vehicle, and the calculation of the steady-state fuel consumption, is best achieved by depicting the vehicle and the engine characteristics as one picture. The relevant engine characteristics are those shown in Fig. 3.5, affording the power output at a number of different throttle angles in conjunction with the related specific fuel consumption contours. The relevant vehicle characteristic is a plot of the power required to drive the vehicle against vehicle speed. The former can be related to the power necessary at the engine flywheel if the overall transmission efficiency is known in the manner described by expression 5.10, except that vehicle speed (V) replaces V_{max}. The latter may be expressed in terms of engine speed if the overall gear ratio is known.

This is shown in Fig. 6.1, in which the power required to propel the medium sized car normally fitted with this 1.6 litre petrol engine

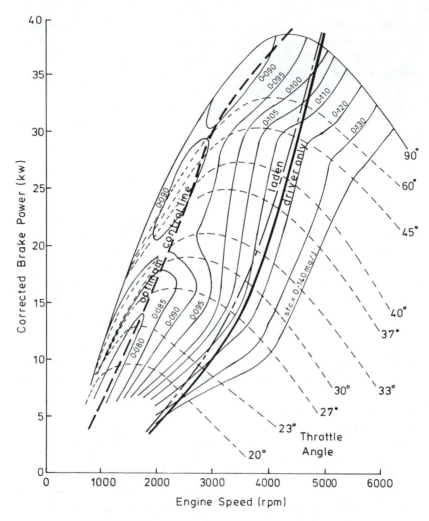

FIGURE 6.1   1.6 litre spark ignition engine characteristics

is superimposed upon the engine characteristics. Two different loading conditions are shown. The first represents the kerb weight of the vehicle with the driver only condition, the second with a full complement of 3 passengers and luggage.

The data relevant to this vehicle are given in Table 6.1, from which it may be shown that the overall gear ratio for top gear is 0.00755

TABLE 6.1
SPECIFICATION OF MEDIUM SIZED SALOON CAR

Mass of vehicle, with driver;	$M_v = 108\,7.7\,kg$
Gear ratios;	3.54, 2.40, 1.41, 1.00
Axle ratio:	$g_a = 3.90$
Rolling radius;	$r_r = 0.281\,m$
Drag coefficients;	$Ad = 0.013, Bd = 0, Cd = 0.49$
Projected frontal area;	$A = 1.858\,m^2$
Tyre growth factor;	$K = 0$

m/s per rev/min of engine speed (0.0169 mile/h per rev/min). Fig 6.1 shows the "driver only" load line to cross the maximum engine power curve at an engine speed of 4900 rev/min. This denotes a maximum vehicle speed of $0.00755 \times 4900 = 36.99$ m/s (133.18 km/h or 82.76 mile/h). A vehicle performance test on this vehicle returned a maximum vehicle speed figure of 83 mile/h.

A notable point is that, in the driver only condition, the vehicle is undergeared, the degree of undergearing being $\lambda = 4900/4300 = 1.14$ and that even in the fully laden state the vehicle is still substantially undergeared. It should be noted also that, while there is power available for acceleration in top gear, as is shown by the vertical difference between the load line and the full power line, the load line is not in close proximity to the optimum control line. It may be that an overdrive drive unit, or a fifth gear, could be employed to advantage, particularly if predominantly motorway travel is expected of the vehicle.

The steps in the calculation of the steady state fuel consumption of the vehicle are outlined in Table 6.2. At particular values of engine speed throughout the top gear running range the vehicle speed may be determined because the overall gear ratio is known. From Fig 6.1, the power required and the corresponding value of specific fuel consumption may be read and hence the rate of fuel consumption in grams/second may be calculated. This may be changed to a volume flow rate of fuel if the relative density of the fuel is known; in this case, 0.740. Dividing the vehicle speed by this volume flow rate of fuel results in the vehicle fuel consumption in km/litre units. The adjacent columns in Table 6.2 show this translated into other common units of expression, of litres/(100 km) and miles/gallon.

From Table 6.2, the fuel curve in Fig. 6.2 may be drawn repre-

TABLE 6.2
FUEL CONSUMPTION OF 1.6 LITRE SALOON CAR (DRIVER ONLY CONDITION)

engine speed rev/min	vehicle speed m/s	power required kw	s.f.c. mg/J	fuel flow rate g/s	fuel flow rate ml/s	Fuel Consumption		
						km/litre	litres 100km	mile/gall
2000	15.07	4.27	0.160	0.683	0.923	16.33	6.13	45.99
2500	18.84	6.82	0.130	0.887	1.199	15.71	6.36	44.26
3000	22.61	10.39	0.117	1.216	1.643	13.76	7.27	38.76
3500	26.38	15.22	0.109	1.659	2.242	11.77	8.50	33.14
4000	30.15	21.54	0.115	2.477	3.347	9.01	11.10	25.37
4500	33.92	29.62	0.105	3.110	4.203	8.07	12.39	22.73
4900	36.93	37.55	0.080	3.000	4.054	9.11	10.98	25.66

senting the calculated steady state fuel consumption of this 1.6 litre, saloon car plotted against vehicle speed. this is to be compared with the dotted line giving the measured fuel consumption of the vehicle. The small difference between the two is a measure of the accuracy to which the steady-state fuel consumption may be estimated from a knowledge of the performance of the engine and the drag coefficients of the vehicle.

The calculated fuel consumption for the 4 people plus luggage loading condition may be dealt with in a similar way. This is not shown on Fig. 6.2 because the line lies close to the driver only loading condition line. The increase in power necessary to drive the vehicle with additional load of course demands an increase in power and hence a possible increase in the fuel flow rate, but this is abated somewhat because the engine is operating at more favourable specific fuel consumptions.

The striking lesson to learn is gained by looking at the steady state fuel consumption which could be returned if the vehicle were fitted

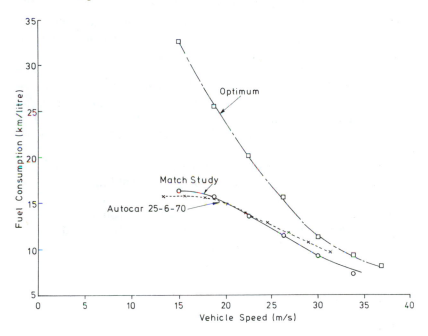

FIGURE 6.2   Fuel consumption 1.6 litre car

with an infinitely variable transmission such that the engine may be controlled on the optimum control line. Table 6.3 sets out the necessary calculations on the assumption that such a transmission may be devised having an identical transmission efficiency to that of a manual transmission. The resulting fuel consumption is denoted by the chain dotted line in Fig. 6.2. This shows a dramatic benefit at low vehicle speeds, a direct result of operating the engine at its best economy for the power output demanded by the vehicle require- ments. It may be seen that this engine operating condition is at a lower engine speed compared with the manual transmission case, resulting in lower engine noise and wear. Some of the gain in fuel consumption is lost at high speed because the load line for the manual transmission is much closer to the optimum control line.

Vehicle acceleration may also be dramatic in that the engine may be taken up the optimum control line to the maximum power output condition in order to achieve the highest possible vehicle acceleration. An infinitely variable transmission need not tie the engine speed to be directly related to the vehicle speed.

Does such a transmission exist? In principle the hydrostatic type, in which the engine drives a hydraulic pump which in turn feeds hydraulic power to hydraulic motors connected to the wheels, is such a transmission. As also are the "friction" drives of the Hayes trans- mission and of the Daf Variomatic. In order to see such a trans- mission installed as standard in a mass produced vehicle, its cost and reliability must be similar to that of a conventional, stepped, trans- mission. Further, the noise and efficiency of the installation must be to acceptable limits.

The Hayes transmission was employed in production Austin cars in the 1930's. Its principle of operation is illustrated in Fig. 6.3. The input drive is connected to two curved discs and the drive transmitted to the double curved disc on the output shaft through rollers. The axes of the rollers may be rotated to provide, in position (1), a 1:1 ratio. In position (2), a speed reduction and hence a torque increase, while position (3) is the "overdrive" position. The transfer of the torque between the curved disc and the roller is through an oil film. Strictly, therefore, the drive is not a friction drive. In order to obtain a sufficient torque transfer, a large clamping force is required between the two input discs.

The belt and sheave type of friction drive, as used in the Daf

TABLE 6.3
FUEL CONSUMPTION WITH AN INFINITELY VARIABLE TRANSMISSION

engine speed rev/min	vehicle speed m/s	power required kw	s.f.c. mg/J	fuel flow rate g/s	fuel flow rate ml/s	Fuel Consumption		
						km/litre	litres 100km	mile/gall
15.07	4.27	820	0.090	0.384	0.519	29.04	3.44	81.79
18.84	6.82	1080	0.085	0.580	0.784	24.03	4.16	67.70
22.61	10.39	1400	0.075	·0.779	1.053	21.47	4.66	60.49
26.38	15.22	1820	0.082	1.248	1.686	15.65	6.39	44.08
30.15	21.54	2360	0.092	1.982	2.678	11.26	8.88	31.72
33.92	29.62	2960	0.085	2.518	3.403	9.97	10.03	28.08
36.93	37.55	4150	0.080	3.004	4.059	9.10	10.99	25.62

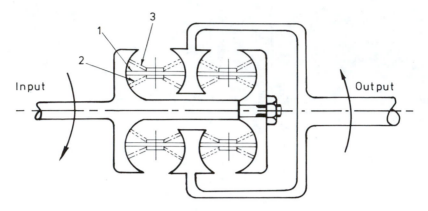

FIGURE 6.3   Hayes transmission

Variomatic transmission, is shown schematically in Fig 6.4. This consists of two expandable V-belt pulleys on the input and output shafts respectively. The drive between the pulleys is through a belt. A control system sets the distance between the flanges of one of the pulleys in accordance with the speed and load requirements. This sets the ratio of the drive.

A simple type of hydrostatic drive is shown diagrammatically in Fig. 6.5. The engine drives a hydraulic pump which delivers fluid at high pressure ($27000kN/m^2$ or, approximately, $4000 lbf/in^2$) to one or more hydraulic motors. Fig. 6.5 shows two motors, one on each of the drive wheels. The differential action is afforded by the tee-junctions in the flow and return pipes. Some arrangements have one motor only with a conventional mechanical drive to the wheels through a propeller shaft and differential gear. However, the system of using tee-junctions in pipework to replace bulky mechanical differential gear lends itself very readily to the provision of a four wheel drive, there being a hydraulic motor at each of the four wheels. Clearly, this system may be easily extended to provide a multi-wheel drive on vehicles having more than four road wheels.

An advantage in replacing a bulky mechanical drive with pipework is that the floor level of the vehicle, and hence its centre of gravity, may be lowered. Further, by fitting hydraulic accumulators to the system, the energy normally lost by the irreversible action of friction brakes may be stored for subsequent usage. This may be achieved by

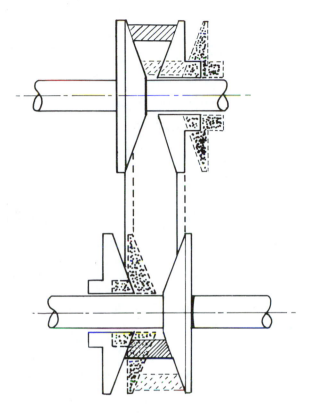

FIGURE 6.4   Belt and sheave friction drive

using the motors as pumps during braking. However, legislation and parking requirements usually demand that friction brakes be fitted as well.

To date, no production motor car is fitted with such a hydrostatic transmission, although their use is commonplace as auxiliary drives on large pieces of machinery and in "off-the-road" vehicles. Their efficiency has been improved in recent years but is still short of the efficiency of a conventional mechanical transmission, particularly when operated at part load. This may be improved by arranging that only a proportion of the power is transmitted hydraulically, as in the "shunt" transmissions described in Chapter 12 or by arranging that not all of the motors are used at part load.

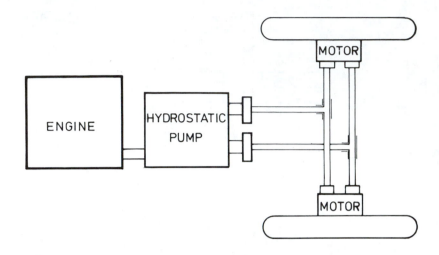

FIGURE 6.5   Hydrostatic transmission

It is apparent therefore that the wide-spread use of the infinitely variable transmission to enable us to operate the engine on its optimum control line is not available yet for motor car use, but that its introduction is by no means an impossibility. There is much development work still to be done on its noise, efficiency, life and reliability.

To return now to the engine characteristics, Fig. 6.1 is typical of the power and specific fuel consumption characteristics of a spark ignition engine. Note how the optimum control line lies quite close to the full power line and constitutes a valley having steep sides in the terrain described by the specific fuel consumption contours.

This is to be compared with Fig 6.6, being the engine characteristics of a typical compression ignition engine. Here we see the optimum control line somewhat removed from the full power line and the specific fuel consumption contours describing a gentle slope on either side of the valley. This feature is characteristic of the difference between the two types of internal combustion engine. The reason for this difference stems from the need to throttle the conventional spark ignition engine in order to control its power output. The mixture strength of the spark ignition engine in its conventional form must be near stoichiometric proportions in order to maintain satisfactory

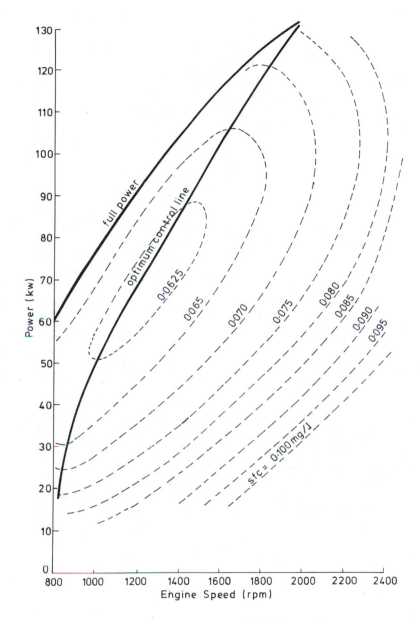

FIGURE 6.6   Compression ignition engine

performance at part load. The compression ignition engine, on the other hand, is not throttled and takes in a full complement of air at part load. To obtain a lower power output, less fuel is injected and the resultant weak mixture burns readily.

The maintenance of a near constant air/fuel ratio by throttling the air at part load results in a high combustion temperature. This leads to a high heat loss to coolant and is the main reason for the poor part load efficiency of the spark ignition engine. This difference between the two types of engine is described in more detail and illustrated by test results elsewhere*. This very important point explains the use of the compression ignition engine in the commercial vehicle field; its part load efficiency being substantially better than that of the spark ignition engine. Efforts are being made to make the spark ignition run satisfactorily at weak mixtures in order that its operating efficiency may be improved.

Turning now to a variation on the conventional spark ignition engine, Fig. 6.7 illustrates the power and efficiency characteristics of a rotary engine of the type epitomised by the name "Wankel".

Note that the optimum control line (not shown) lies close to the full power line in the manner characteristic of the spark ignition engine. The labels on the specific fuel consumption contours are in the imperial units in which the data was collected, however, in order that a comparison may be made, the appropriate S.I. values are given in brackets.

Superimposed onto Fig. 6.7 is the load line of the small sports car the engine normally powers. This shows the overall gearing to be neutral, neither undergeared or overgeared.

The overall top gear ratio of this vehicle is 0.016 mile/h per rev/min giving a calculated maximum vehicle speed of 92.7 mile/h. This compares well with the figure of 92 mile/h measured during a performance test. Fig. 6.8 is a graph of the resultant calculated fuel consumption of this small sports car compared with values measured during a performance test on the vehicle. The agreement is excellent for the majority of the speed range, though the fuel consumption figures themselves are rather poor for such a small vehicle.

Fig 6.9 shows schematically the layout of a contender for the

---

*Greene, A.B. and Lucas, G.G. "The Testing of Internal Combustion Engines" The English Universities Press.

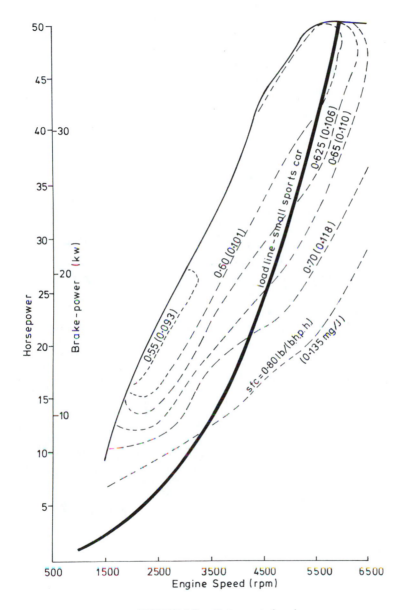

FIGURE 6.7   Rotary petrol engine

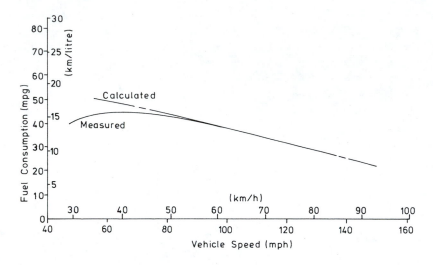

FIGURE 6.8   Fuel consumption of small sports car fitted with rotary engine

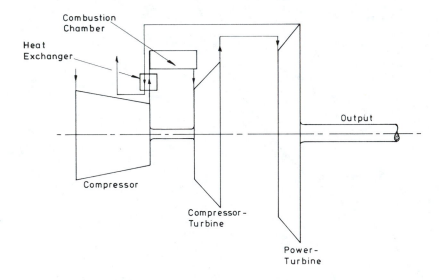

FIGURE 6.9   Schematic of automotive gas turbine

propulsion unit for road vehicles; the gas turbine in its free power turbine configuration. This has a good torque curve for traction purposes, the torque rising as the output shaft speed decreases to give a maximum torque output of 2 to 3 times the full speed torque at an output shaft speed of zero. Thus, as the load on the engine increases and reduces the free power turbine speed the torque output is capable of rising to meet this increase in load. This capability stems from the fact that the speed of the gas generator portion of the engine, that is the compressor and compressor turbine, may be independent of the free turbine speed. It may therefore be run at its maximum speed producing near constant power in the gas flow to the free power turbine. The torque curve we see therefore is that of a "constant power" engine, like the reciprocating steam engine, factored by the poorer efficiency of the turbine as we move way from the design point.

Fig. 6.10 is a graph of the power output of a 350 hp gas turbine designed for use in a road vehicle. The lines of constant fuel flow rate correspond to fixed gas generator speeds; the $\dot{m}_f = 139$ lb/h figure representing the maximum speed of the compressor, the 117 lb/h figure representing 95 % of maximum speed. Similarly, the other fuel flow rates shown on Fig. 6.10 represent 90 %, 80 %, 70 %, 50 % and idle compressor speeds. The data contained in Fig. 6.10 may be re-arranged to give the specific fuel consumption curves. These, in turn, may be cross-plotted onto the power curves in the manner outlined above to give Fig. 6.11.

The power and specific fuel consumption curves of the automotive gas turbine engine present a different picture to those of the recipro-cating engines. The valley of the optimum control line is considerably removed from the full power line. Superimposed onto Fig. 6.11 is the load line of a 38 ton truck, the overall gearing having been arranged to be neutral. This may be seen to be virtually coincident with the optimum control line for much of its length.

This redeeming feature of the gas turbine characteristics presents a rather better prospect than is usually put forward for this engine and emphasizes that it is of little value to look at the efficiency figure down the full power curve in order to draw conclusions on its suit-ability to power a vehicle. This, as is well known, shows the thermal efficiency of the gas turbine engine to fall rapidly below the half power mark. A full match study between the engine and the vehicle

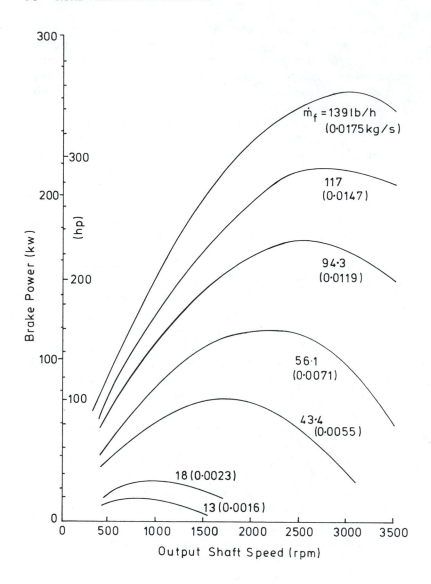

FIGURE 6.10   Gas turbine power curves

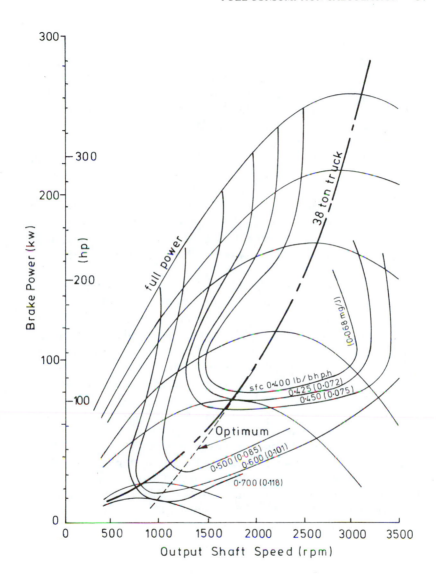

FIGURE 6.11   Gas turbine engine characteristics

on the other hand shows the efficiency figures to be not too bad right down to quite low powers.

The optimum control line of the automotive gas turbine engine takes a path through the maximum power points on the curves in Fig. 6.11, the reason being that the maximum efficiency points and the maximum power points are coincident. Should the free power turbine be capable of transmitting the power input to it in the form of a high energy gas stream into shaft power with 100% efficiency throughout its speed range, the power curves in Fig. 6.10 would be horizontal lines reflecting the constant power input at each of the gas generator speeds. But a turbine, particularly a turbine housing fixed geometry blading, is not capable of maintaining a high efficiency throughout its speed range. The efficiency falls off quite rapidly either side of the design point; the speed best suited to the blade angles. The power curves in Fig. 6.10 therefore follow the shape of the turbine efficiency curves.

It follows therefore that the shape of the locus through the maxima of the efficiency curves, and hence the optimum control line, is determined by the detail design of the engine, particularly of the blade angles. It may therefore be modified to suit a particular application. This point should be studied very carefully at the design stage of a gas turbine because the point at which a gas turbine compressor begins to surge, that is to exhibit an unstable flow pattern, may be approached under low load conditions.

We have seen in the above the shapes of the power and efficiency characteristics of several types of engine and we have seen that these, in conjunction with information on the drag of the vehicles, may be used to calculate the steady-state fuel consumption of the vehicle. This information is, of itself, extremely useful and may well be all that is required. However, there remains this problem mentioned earlier of the prediction of the overall fuel consumption of a vehicle, entailing the effects of transient conditions.

Some idea of the effect of transients on final consumption may be obtained from Fig. 6.12, taken from a Organisation for Economic Co-operation and Development (OECD) report entitled, "Automobile fuel consumption in actual traffic conditions" dated December 1981. The vertical scale is in terms of litres per 100 km which is proportional to the reciprocal of the scale used in the figures above. However, the message is clear that the lower the average speed, due

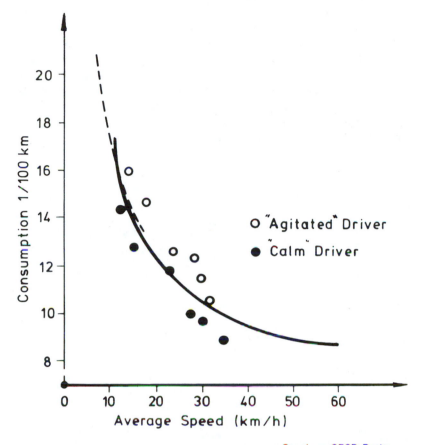

FIGURE 6.12   Fuel consumption in urban area as a function of average speed

to travel congestion and other phenomena causing transient effects, the greater the difference between the actual fuel consumption and that measured and predicted under steady state conditions.

The type of duty of the motor vehicle therefore is clearly important, but then so is the type of driver as can be seen in Fig. 6.12. It is well known that different drivers can return very different fuel consumptions from the same vehicle. This difference is considerably larger than the tolerance one would expect on the accuracy of a theoretical prediction. It is questionable therefore if it is worthwhile to attempt such predictions. The results of a very large amount of computation to cater for the many transient effects should be compared to the steady-state fuel consumption anyway to be meaningful. It may be argued then that it is preferable to relate the overall fuel consumption to the steady state using some rule-of-thumb technique based upon experience. Fig. 6.12 points the way to such a technique in that it contains a suggestion as to the form of an expression that might be used as the basis.

7 Parametric Study

The technique of predicting the steady-state fuel consumption of a vehicle developed in Chapter 6 and the maximum speed and accelerative performance calculations of Chapter 5 may be used to gain a measure of the effect of various design and operating parameters upon vehicle performance. This type of exercise is usually in response to the Designer's query, "What would happen if -----?" For instance, what is the incentive to reduce vehicle weight? Is it important to keep it low?; because to do so may involve considerable design time. Similarly, it may be reasoned that it is desirable to have some notional indication of the effect of the overall gear ratio, of the aerodynamic drag and, say, of engine size. By using the techniques already developed, these and other effects may be predicted at the design state.

This chapter therefore is devoted to a study of the main parameters detailed above, of vehicle weight, overall gear ratio, aerodynamic drag and engine size on the steady-state fuel consumption and on maximum speed and accelerative performance. Typical vehicle sizes are used from which it is suggested that the results from the particular may be used to infer general conclusions.

First, let us consider the effect of the weight of a small petrol engined car upon fuel consumption. Fig. 7.1 depicts the characteristics of the engine upon which are superimposed three load lines. The first, shown short dashed, is the normal load line of the vehicle showing it to have a degree of undergearing of $\lambda \simeq 1$. The other two lines are the load lines of the vehicle with a 20 % increase in weight. There are two such load lines because the weight may be added as a result of two distinct actions. These are that the vehicle owner may add weight in the form of luggage or passengers etc. or conversely, the vehicle manufacturer may have allowed the vehicle to be heavier than is desirable. If the latter is the case, then the overall gear ratio must be modified accordingly to bring it back to $\lambda \simeq 1$ in order to

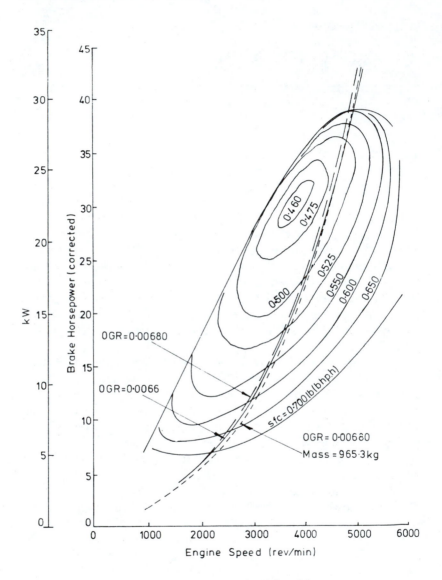

FIGURE 7.1   Effect of vehicle weight

effect a comparison. Of the two additional load lines representing the 20% increase in weight, the long dashed line is with no change in the overall gear ratio (the owner adds the weight) and the other, the full line, is with a commensurate change in the overall gear ratio to maintain unity degree of undergearing (the manufacturer is responsible for the weight increase). The normal kerb weight of this car is 9466 N (mass = 965.3 kg) with an overall gear ratio of 0.00680 m/s per rev/min (0.0245 km/h or 0.0152 mile/h per rev/min). This must be changed to 0.00666 m/s per rev/min if the 20% increase in weight is added as a result of the vehicle design.

Fig. 7.2 shows the steady-state fuel consumption for the three cases. Increasing the weight of a petrol engined vehicle has a small effect only throughout the normal speed range. Moving the load line towards the overgeared side rapidly accrues the benefits from the steep slope of the specific fuel consumption contours. Even though the weight of the vehicle, and hence its rolling resistance, has increased, the small change in steady-state fuel consumption may even be to the good, as in this case.

This accords with experience. A car on a long run, say during vacation time, may have a load considerably greater than that carried

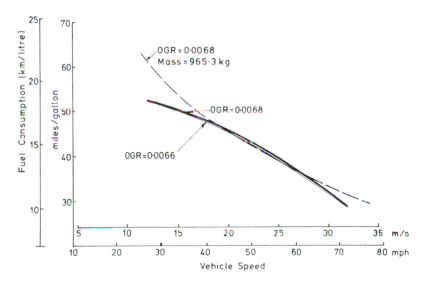

FIGURE 7.2   Fuel consumption, effect of vehicle weight

normally for its "about town" running. This increase consisting of a full family with its luggage compared with, say, the driver-only condition for the normal every-day running. Usually, on such a run, the fuel consumption is better than the about-town running by a significant amount provided that a roof rack is not employed, even though the average speed of the car is substantially higher. The reason is mainly due to the lack of transients but it illustrates the small effect only of the increase in car weight.

Changing the overall gear ratio in order to maintain a near unity degree of undergearing does have a small detrimental effect on the steady-state fuel consumption but, of course, the acceleration improves and, to a very small extent, so does the maximum speed of the vehicle.

A similar exercise on a compression ignition engined commercial vehicle however produces a rather different conclusion. Fig. 7.3 shows the characteristics of a 11.1 litre compression ignition engine upon which have been superimposed the load lines of a 23 ton truck. The short dashed line, marked 5.87 kw/(100.kg) (8.0 hp/ton) is the normal load line while the long dashed and full lines are the load lines for a 25 % reduction in weight, the former with no change in the overall gear ratio and the latter with a change in order to return the degree of undergearing to near unity. The corresponding steady-state fuel consumption curves are given in Fig. 7.4. These show a significant change in fuel consumption with vehicle weight; the 25 % reduction resulting in a reduction in fuel consumption of some 20 %. Again, the more overgeared line returning a slightly better fuel consumption.

The reason for the marked difference in fuel consumption with vehicle weight in the case of the compression ignition engine lies in the low slope of the specific fuel consumption contours. As the load line is moved as a result of a change in vehicle weight, the change in engine specific fuel consumption is small and does not mitigate seriously against the other factor of the change, that of the power required to propel the vehicle. In the case of a petrol engined vehicle, the effects of these two factors are finely balanced to result in little change in fuel consumption with a change in vehicle weight of the order of 20 %. However, it can be shown that a massive change in weight, such as that caused by fully ladening a petrol engined commercial vehicle, does result in a considerable change in fuel

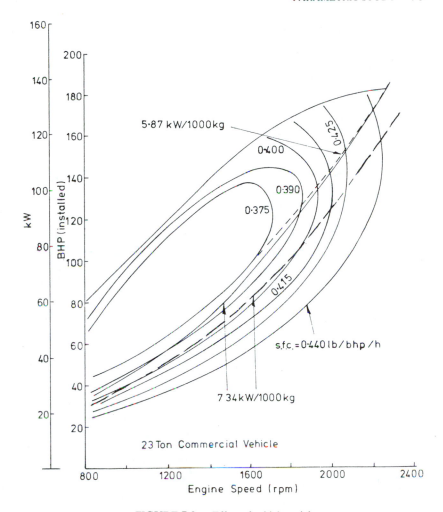

FIGURE 7.3   Effect of vehicle weight

consumption, particularly at low vehicle speeds.

The change in the overall gear ratio with vehicle weight in order to maintain near unity degree of undergearing is an indication of the effect of weight upon vehicle maximum speed. To look at this further the calculation procedure for vehicle maximum speed developed in Chapter 5 may be used. This, for a similar 1 litre petrol engined car to that used above, results in the effect shown in Fig. 7.5 and suggests

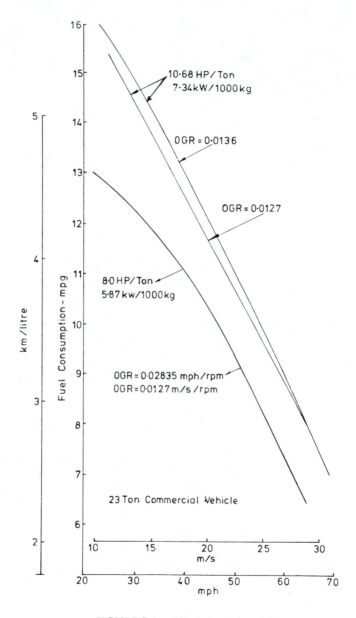

FIGURE 7.4   Effect of vehicle weight

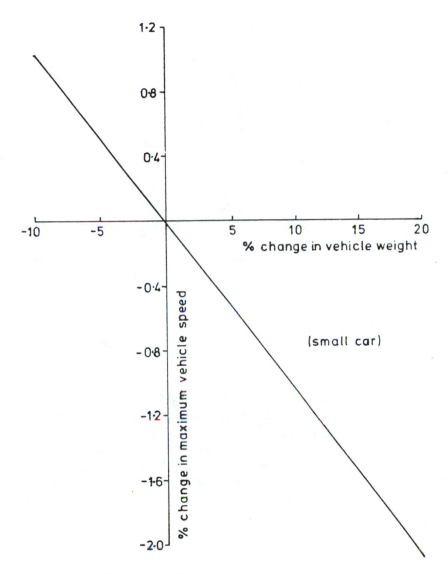

FIGURE 7.5   Effect of vehicle weight on maximum speed

that a 10% change in car weight results in a 1% change approximately in maximum speed.

Similarly, the technique outlined in Chapter 5 for the calculation of the time-to-speed of a vehicle may be used to assess the effect of vehicle weight. Again, taking this 1 litre car as an example results in the curves given in Fig. 7.6. When the final speed is low, say up to 20 m/s (72 km/h, 44.7 mile/h), a near linear relationship exists between time-to-speed and vehicle weight. The near linear relationship is because the drag, consisting mainly of rolling resistance at such low speeds, is nearly proportional to vehicle weight. As the final speed in the integration process is increased the relationship becomes less linear. Fig. 7.6 suggests that a 10% reduction in car weight may result in a similar change in the time to cruise speed.

Altering the axle ratio of a vehicle in order to change the degree of undergearing from a large amount of undergear to a large amount of overgear results, typically, in Fig. 7.7, giving the steady-state fuel consumption for the 1 litre car and in Fig. 7.8 for the 23 ton commercial vehicle. These show that overgearing a vehicle does decrease the fuel consumption but that a law of diminishing returns operates for both the petrol engined car and the compression ignition engined truck.

This effect has to be compromised with the reduction in accelerative performance as the overgearing is increased. Fig. 7.9 depicts the calculated percentage change in time-to-speed of the 1 litre car against the percentage change in axle ratio for four final speeds in the integration process. This shows that undergearing does result in an improvement in accelerative performance but that there exists a curious minimum on the overgeared side which alters its position as the final speed in the integration process is altered. This minimum is a result of the overgearing being such that it is not necessary to change into top gear before reaching the final speed in the integration process. As the axle ratio is altered towards the undergeared side a gear change becomes necessary with the attendant loss in accelerative performance in the vacinity of the gear change speed. This, it should be noted, is with the assumption that the gear change time is zero.

This feature is only of some significance if the time to a particular final speed is the predominant parameter of accelerative performance and, of course, in general this is not so. It does however illustrate the importance of the point made in Chapter 5 that it is undesirable to

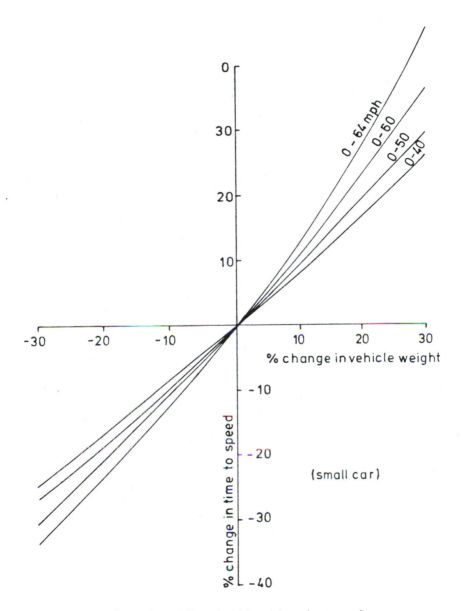

FIGURE 7.6   Effect of vehicle weight on time to speed

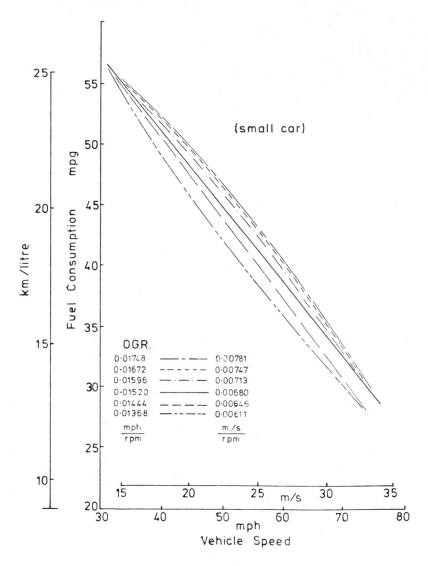

FIGURE 7.7   Effect of overall gear ratio

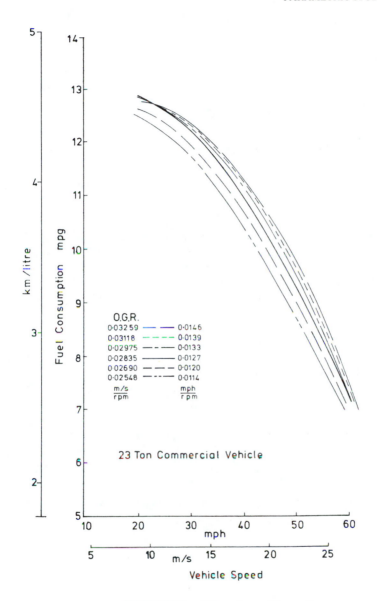

FIGURE 7.8   Effect of overall fear ratio

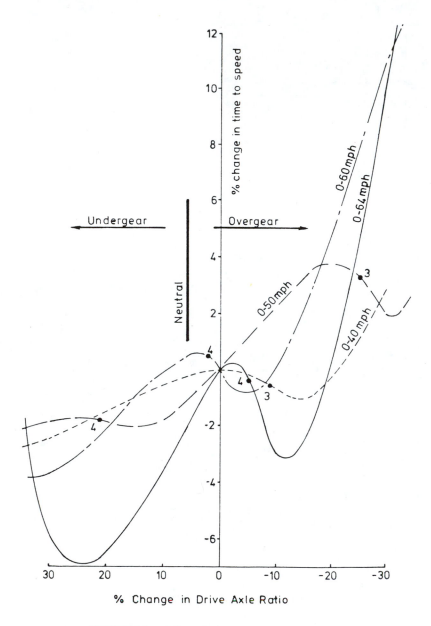

FIGURE 7.9   Effect of drive axle ratio on time to speed

attempt to pre-specify the gear change speeds. The computer program must be capable of working these out itself.

The effect of axle ratio on maximum speed of a small car may be seen in Fig. 7.10. The neutral gearing condition affords the greatest maximum speed, but the fall off either side is slight reflecting the small change in engine power either side of the maximum power speed.

It may be concluded therefore that axle ratio is a careful compromise between fuel consumption and accelerative performance. Alternatively, the vehicle is provided with a special gear ratio to cater for one or both of these performance criteria.

The gains to be made from reducing the aerodynamic drag coefficient lie in the reduced fuel consumption, rather than in dramatic changes in accelerative performance. Figs. 7.11 and 7.12 contain the calculated steady-state fuel consumptions of the 1 litre car and the 23 ton truck respectively. The axle ratios have been modified with the change in Cd in order to maintain a constant degree of undergearing. Three Cd values have been considered in both cases, the normal Cd of the vehicle, an increase of 25% and a decrease of 25%. These show a significant gain in fuel consumption by paying careful attention to the aerodynamic shape of a vehicle. The gain is slightly more with the car because the bulk of the drag force of a truck is rolling resistance. Nevertheless, the savings to be made on the truck are well worth having.

Much can be done to decrease the aerodynamic drag of a new design of vehicle. Corners should be well rounded in the plan view and in the front and side elevations. Protruding structures should be avoided. A common culprit for increased fuel consumption is the luggage rack on the roof of a motor car. It is not generally realised that this can nearly double the aerodynamic drag of the vehicle; by an increase in the aerodynamic drag coefficient and by an increase in the projected frontal area. A motorway journey of 100 miles can cost an extra gallon of petrol if a roof rack is fitted.

The effect of the aerodynamic drag coefficient on the accelerative performance of a vehicle on the other hand is not nearly so marked. The full line in Fig. 7.13 gives the calculated time-to-speed of a 2 litre saloon car at its normal aerodynamic drag coefficient of Cd = 0.428. The dotted line gives the calculated time-to-speed when this is reduced to Cd = 0.320, a value that can be achieved practically.

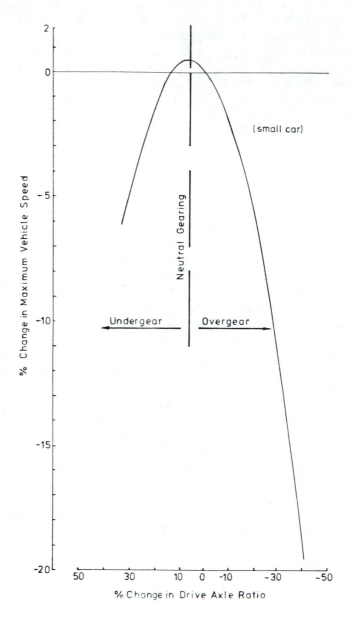

FIGURE 7.10   Effect of drive axle ratio maximum speed

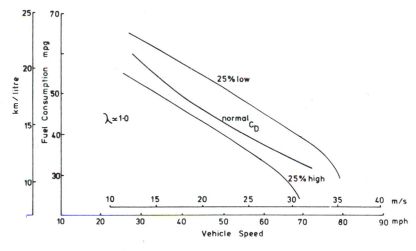

FIGURE 7.11   Effect of C_D (small car)

There is virtually no difference in the times until quite a high speed is attained. However the maximum speed is increased from 45.6 m/s (164.1 km/h, 102 mile/h) to 48.7 m/s (175.4 km/h, 109 mile/h), an increase of nearly 7%.

The reason for the little difference in accelerative performance throughout the lower half of the speed range is that, in the lower gears, there is a considerable accelerative force, such that a change in just the aerodynamic drag component, itself a function of speed, makes little difference. However, it effects the maximum vehicle speed and the fuel consumption to a considerable extent. It is clear therefore that attention to the aerodynamic drag coefficient should pay dividends.

In the consideration of the effect of engine size, of course, we can say straight away that a larger and more powerful engine will return a better time-to-speed and a higher maximum speed. This is obvious; but it is worth remembering that it requires a considerable increase in power to raise the maximum speed significantly because the power required to propel a vehicle varies with approximately the cube of speed. The effect of engine size therefore is largely a study of its effect on the steady-state fuel consumption.

The first point to note is that an increase in the power output does not necessarily result in a deterioration in fuel consumption, although

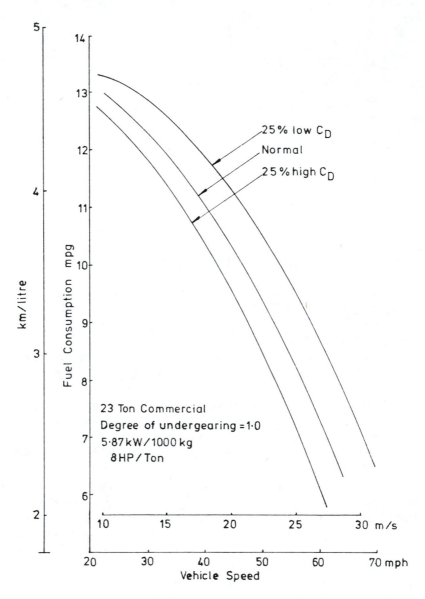

FIGURE 7.12 Effect of C_D

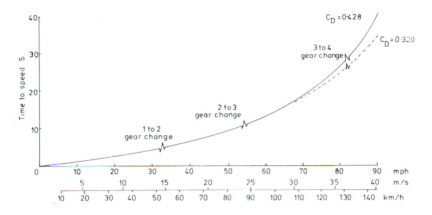

FIGURE 7.13   Effect of reducing C on time to speed

this is usually the case. Consider the 1 litre motor car cited above fitted first with its usual 4 cylinder petrol engine having one carburetter and then fitted with the same engine equipped with two carburetters. The latter condition affording an increase in power output. Figs. 7.14 and 7.15 show the load line of this vehicle superimposed upon the two engine characteristics. Fig. 7.16 contains the curves of the resulting steady-state fuel consumptions. The twin carburetter version of the engine is the better match to this particular vehicle.

All engine designs are different. Each has its own peculiarities, such that it is difficult to stretch the power axis of the characteristics of a particular engine and say that this is what the characteristics would look like if the engine were larger. However, to some extent, general conclusions on the effect of engine size may be drawn by studying the steady-state fuel consumption returned from a theoretical assessment of a vehicle powered by three particular spark ignition engines in turn. These three engines are of the same manufacturer and are of similar, though not identical, design. Their sizes are 0.843, 1.221 and 2.100 litres respectively and, for the purposes of this study, are matched to the same small car used elsewhere in this chapter. The degree of undergearing in each case has been arranged to be unity.

Fig. 7.17 shows the calculated steady-state fuel consumption for this vehicle with each of three engines. A relatively small, but notice-

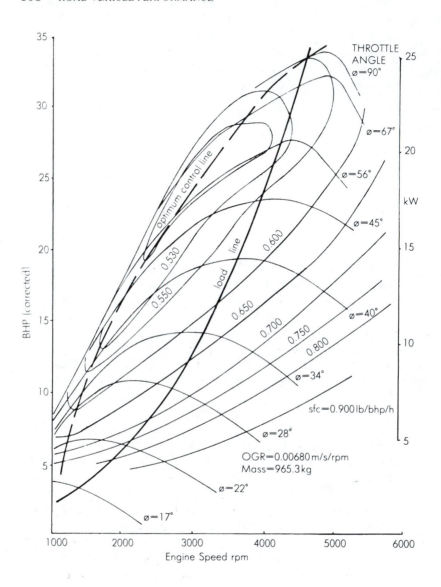

FIGURE 7.14   Small car — one carburetter

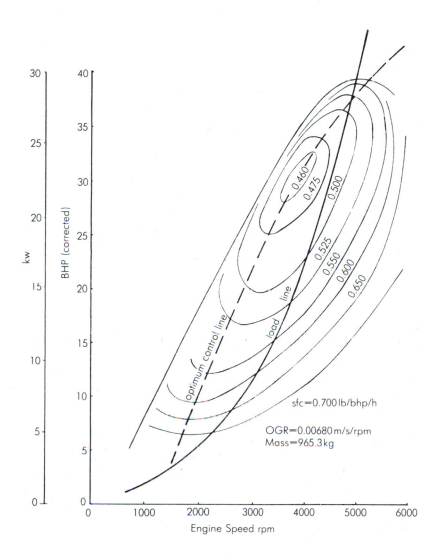

FIGURE 7.15   Small car — two carburetters

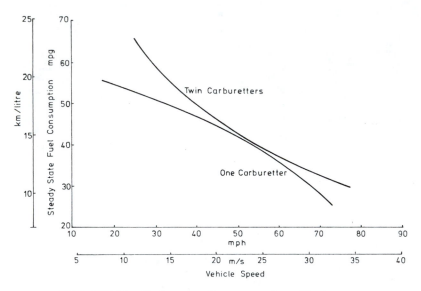

FIGURE 7.16   Fuel consumption — comparison of intake systems

able difference is apparent between the 1.221 and the 2.100 litre engines, the two curves drawing together at the higher vehicle speeds. The curve of the small 0.843 litre engine however, shows a large gain at low vehicle speeds which diminishes rapidly as the vehicle speed is increased such that, at 29 m/s (104.6 km/h, 65 miles/h), the larger 1.221 litre engine returns a better fuel consumption.

A similar exercise on the 23 ton commercial vehicle has produced very similar conclusions and although it would be unsafe to be dogmatic in generalising from the particular in this case, there is an indication that too small an engine will produce economy at low speeds but may lose at higher speeds. The real conclusion is that the engine should be carefully matched to the vehicle at the design stage.

Having looked at the effect of the main design and operating parameters on vehicle performance one could continue to investigate the effect of rolling resistance, tyre growth, wind speed, ambient pressure and temperature, "under-bonnet" temperature, road wheel inertia, engine inertia, the gear ratios, gradient etc., etc. This list emphasizes the value of theoretical models of this nature in that, while the results may not accord exactly with practical tests, they can be made to predict the right trends and so point the way for the

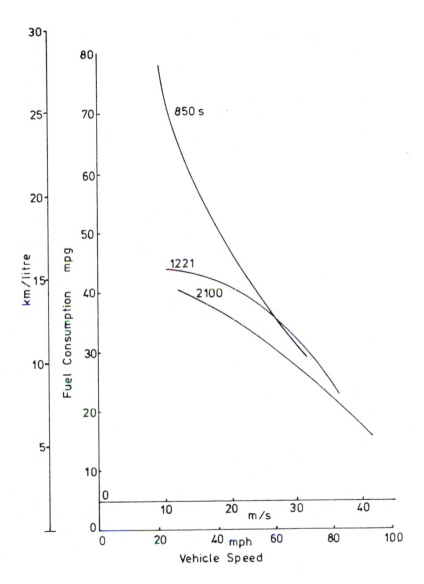

FIGURE 7.17   Effect of engine size

designer. As an illustration of this, this chapter is concluded with a description of a technique for correcting experimental time-to-speed results for ambient pressure, temperature and steady wind speed. In the development of this correction technique, a computer time-to-speed program was used in conjunction with the specifications of five motor cars ranging from a small low powered vehicle to a high powered sports car. This was in preference to the use of experimental results with their element of driver behaviour and interaction of several parameters. Some experimental results were used however to relate the under-bonnet temperature, that is the temperature of the air entering the engine intake, to ambient temperature. Tests on three different cars suggest that the underbonnet temperature approaches the ambient temperature as the vehicle speed is increased and that the difference between the two may be expressed as a third order polynomial

$$T_{ub} - T_o = 28.0 - 1.6.V + 0.035.V^2 - 0.00034.V^3 \qquad 7.1$$

where T_{ub} (°K) is the underbonnet temperature, T_o (°K) is the ambient temperature and V (m/s) is the vehicle speed.

From computations of the time-to-speed for the five cars, the experimental time-to-speed with a head wind (t_h) and the time-to-speed in the opposite direction (t_t) may be corrected to give the time-to-speed which would have resulted had there been zero wind speed, as follows

$$t_w = \frac{4.V.t_h.t_t}{(t_h).(2.V + V_w) + (t_t).(2.V - V_w)} \qquad 7.2$$

where V_w is the steady head-on wind speed and V is the particular vehicle speed. It has been found that simply to average the times-to-speed resulting from runs in opposite directions when there is a steady wind speed in the direction of the track produces very misleading results. Although if the wind speed is not too high, this averaging procedure is acceptable with maximum speed measurements.

In the case of time-to-speed tests with a wind speed in the direction of the track the procedure should be therefore to conduct two runs in opposite directions and, for each discrete velocity between zero and the final speed, note the corresponding times (t_h) and (t_t). These are then used in expression 7.2 to give the corrected time to each of the discrete speeds (V). These data of t_w against V may be further corrected for temperature and pressure to give the time-to-speed which would prevail on a standard day having an ambient pressure Ps and an ambient temperature T_S. The latter may be used in expression 7.1 to give the under-bonnet temperature on a standard day. The corrected time-to-speed V is given by

$$t_c = t_w \left[\frac{A - B.V^2}{C - D.V^2} \right] \qquad 7.3$$

This expression is simple in form and easy to apply, but it does involve the prior determination of some awkward constants. They are

$$A = E \frac{Po}{Ps} \sqrt{\frac{Ts}{T_{ub}}} - 0.0331.M_v \qquad 7.4$$

$$B = \frac{\frac{2248.P_{max}}{V_{max}} \frac{Po}{Ps} \sqrt{\frac{Ts}{T_{ub}}} - 0.0331.M_v}{V_{max}^2} \qquad 7.5$$

$$C = E - 0.0331.M_v \qquad 7.6$$

$$D = \frac{\frac{224.8.P_{max}}{V_{max}} - 0.0031.M_v}{V_{max}^2} \qquad 7.7$$

$$\text{and } E = 2147 \times \frac{P_{max}}{N_p} \times \frac{0.95 \times g_g \times g_a}{r_r} \qquad 7.8$$

where P_o and P_s are the observed and standard ambient pressures, T_{ub} and T_s are the actual under-bonnet and standard temperatures, M_v (kg) is the vehicle mass, P_{max} (kw) is the maximum power output of the engine under standard conditions and V_{max} (m/s) is an estimation of the maximum speed of the vehicle. N_p (rev/min) is the maximum power speed of the engine, g_g is the appropriate gear ratio, g_a is the axle ratio and r_r the rolling radius of the wheels.

The expressions above are based upon the premise that the product of vehicle acceleration and time remains a constant for all environmental conditions. This has been developed to produce this correction technique and another, more sophisticated, technique designed for use with more sophisticated test instrumentation. This second technique assumes that the time-to-speed test data are processed by computer. Each data point is factored by the ratio of the results of a time-to-speed computer program fed with the standard test conditions and with those of the day of the test. These two correction procedures are described in detail and their accuracy analysed in a paper by the Author and his colleagues to the 2nd International Conference on Vehicle Mechanics held in Paris, September 1971, entitled "Correction for the effect of ambient conditions on vehicle time-to-speed results". This shows that it is necessary to correct time-to-speed results if they are to be meaningful.

The parametric study of this chapter illustrates the usefulness of vehicle performance calculation techniques in the provision of guidance on the effect of vehicle design and operating parameters. A particular use has been outlined in the development of a correction technique for changes in environmental conditions; a technique which would have been very difficult from experimental data.

8 Fixing the Gear Ratios

The use of theoretical vehicle performance techniques in parametric studies inevitably suggests that a rational system be specified for fixing the number of and the values of the gear ratios in a manual transmission. In altering a parameter through a wide range in order to study its effect it may be that the normal gear ratios for the vehicle are inadequate. Indeed, the vehicle specification itself may be so remote that no previous experience exists upon which to draw in the fixing of the ratios. Normally, a designer relies heavily on past experience for this task. There is nothing wrong in this; it is a very sound and reliable design technique to use the criticism of existing designs to better future design. If the new design of vehicle is not too different from previous models, an experienced designer can simply write down an effective set of gear ratios. This does not help us however when conducting theoretical studies; this experience may not exist even if the specification is conventional. This chapter therefore examines philosophies for the determination of the gear ratios and develops a technique which may be incorporated into a time-to-speed computer program as an "optional extra" in that the program could be asked to fix the gear ratios rather than that they be specified in the input data.

Let us start with the top gear ratio because this is reasonably straight-forward. It hinges simply on the compromise between good top gear acceleration and fuel economy, that is on the specification of the degree of undergearing. Once the designer has decided this he has effectively fixed the overall top gear ratio. The maximum speed of the vehicle is calculated in the manner outlined at the end of chapter 5. From this, and the definition of the degree of undergearing, the overall top gear ratio (G) may be obtained:

$$G = \frac{V_{max}}{N_\rho \times \lambda} \qquad\qquad 8.1$$

The product of the top gear ratio and the axle ratio is given by using the expression for the overall gear ratio, viz:

$$g_{g(top)} \times g_a = \frac{2\pi}{60} \times \frac{(t_r)_{Vmax}}{G} \qquad\qquad 8.2$$

These two ratios are lumped together as a product because, frequently, the fixing of the top gear ratio is really the fixing of the axle ratio. It being usual to design the gear box such that, in the often used top gear, the input shaft is connected directly to the output shaft in order to avoid the transmission of power through gears. The top gear ratio ($g_{g(top)}$) therefore is often unity and expression 8.2 afford the value of the axle ratio (g_a).

The decision on the value of the degree of undergearing to use in order to fix the overall top gear ratio is usually not too difficult. Top gear acceleration has to be balanced against fuel economy together with engine noise and life, when in doubt, a safe course is to take the degree of undergearing (λ) to be equal to unity. However, one may wish to have the best of both sides and to arrange for the provision of an "overdrive" gear. This special gear ratio, which may be incorporated into the design of the gearbox or which may be embodied in a separate unit in the drive line, is engaged during cruise conditions and arranges the vehicle to be substantially overgeared. For acceleration purposes, the overdrive unit may be disengaged, usually by the simple touching of a switch. With such a unit therefore, the normal top gear ratio may be fixed such that the vehicle is somewhat undergeared.

There are shades of opinion however in the manner in which the bottom gear ratio should be fixed. All are agreed that the functions of this ratio are in moving the vehicle from rest and in climbing steep gradients and that, from the theoretical standpoint, these two functions are virtually synonymous; a high initial acceleration being broadly equivalent to good gradeability.

Some say that the vehicle should be capable of scaling a particular gradient, which, for a motor car, is usually $33\frac{1}{3}\%$ (1 in 3) or 25% (1 in 4). This ignores the fact that gradients exist which are steeper. This is true for the public road system of course, but one need not go far to find steep gradients. Some ramps up to car ferries and driveways to private houses can be very steep. Further, one should bear in mind that the vehicle may have additional load to the norm; in fact it may be towing a caravan or trailer. However, using this criterion, the bottom gear ratio is arranged such that the maximum torque of the engine is translated into a force at the wheels equal and opposite to the downhill component of the vehicle weight. That is that:

$$T_{max} \times \frac{g_{g(1st)} \times g_a}{r_r} \times \eta_T = W.i \qquad 8.3$$

from which by setting the transmission efficiency (η_T) at, say, 0.90, the first gear ratio $g_{g(1st)}$ may be fixed. This means that the vehicle should be capable of negotiating the specified gradient (i) provided that it is in first gear and moving at such a speed that its engine speed is above the maximum torque speed.

It is a rather different matter if the specification for the design of bottom gear stipulates that the vehicle must be capable of starting from rest on a stated gradient (usually i = 0.25). In order to fix bottom gear ratio from this criterion the equations of motion of the two subsystems depicted in Figure 4.3 must be solved, they are:

$$\frac{d\omega_e}{dt} = \frac{T_e - T_c}{I_e} \qquad 8.4$$

$$\text{and } \frac{d\omega_v}{dt} = \frac{T_c - T_v}{I_v} \qquad 8.5$$

where ω = rotational speed (rad/s), T = torque (Nm), I = inertia and t = time (s). Suffices e denotes the engine side, v the vehicle side and c denotes the clutch.

The first describes the engine side of the clutch and the second the vehicle side, the inertias in the latter being related to clutch output speed. These equations may be solved and the motion of the vehicle described if the engine initial speed, the variation of engine torque, the friction characteristics of the clutch and the manner in which the coefficient of friction varies with slip speed and temperature and, finally, the manner in which the driver operates the clutch are known. This latter point is very necessary if realistic predictions of vehicle take-off on a gradient are to be made. A driver slips the clutch in quite a distinctive manner when moving off from rest, particularly when on a steep gradient. Typically, as illustrated in Figure 8.1, he applies just sufficient clamp load to move the vehicle and holds this until the clutch slip is near to zero. He then applies the remaining clamp load rapidly.

The description of this, in the form

$$\frac{dP}{dt} = \text{a specified function}$$ 8.6

with differential equations describing the heat generation and transfer, together with equations 8.4 and 8.5 may be solved analytically

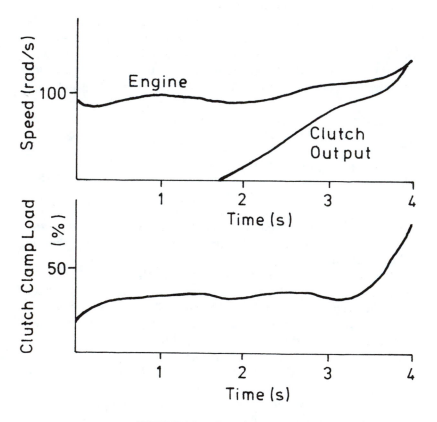

FIGURE 8.1   Clutch engagement

using a suitable integration technique. Quite a formidable task, and for what advantage?

Suppose we mentally increase the slope the vehicle is asked to climb from a low value to a very high value. Clearly, we can continue to lower the bottom gear ratio to provide sufficient force at the drive wheels to oppose the downhill component of the vehicle weight. Does this mean therefore that the vehicle can then scale a vertical wall? The answer, of course, is "No". Long before this situation is reached the drive wheels would lose adhesion with the road surface. Suppose therefore we mentally increase the slope and arrange bottom gear ratio to provide sufficient force at the drive wheels until this limiting condition of wheel-spin is encountered. If we stop there we have done the best we can in terms of the gradeability of the vehicle. Purely arbitrary values of $i = 0.333$ or $i = 0.25$ therefore are not relevant. We have fixed the bottom gear ratio such that the vehicle may climb the maximum gradient that it is possible for it to climb, without wheel-spin.

If we assume zero vehicle acceleration on the gradient and that the coefficient of friction between tyres and road is unity, Fig. 4.1 shows the limiting tractive force to be, in the case of a rear wheel drive vehicle

$$F_l = \frac{W}{(a + b)} (a.\mathrm{Cos}\theta + h.\mathrm{Sin}\theta) \qquad 8.7$$

and, for a front wheel drive vehicle

$$F_l = \frac{W}{(a + b)} (b.\mathrm{Cos}\theta - h.\mathrm{Sin}\theta) \qquad 8.8$$

Equating this limiting tractive force to the downhill component of the vehicle weight (W),

i.e. $F_l = W.\mathrm{Sin}\,\theta$ \qquad 8.9

yields

$$\theta = \text{Tan}^{-1} \left(\frac{a}{a+b-h} \right) \qquad\qquad 8.10$$

for a rear wheel drive vehicle and

$$\theta = \text{Tan}^{-1} \left(\frac{b}{a+b+h} \right) \qquad\qquad 8.11$$

for a front wheel drive vehicle.

Repeating this exercise for the case of a all-wheel drive vehicle results in a maximum slope of $\theta = 45°$ (i = 0.7071, or 1 in 1.414)

The maximum gradient therefore that it is possible for a vehicle to climb is a function of the position of the centre of gravity. In passing, it should be noted that, for a 50/50 weight distribution (i.e. a = b), a rear wheel vehicle may scale a steeper gradient than a front wheel drive vehicle and that both have less gradeability than the all-wheel drive vehicle.

Having found the maximum possible slope we arrange bottom gear ratio to provide sufficient force at the drive wheels to meet this condition. That is that:

$$g_{g(1st)} = W.\text{Sin}\theta \times \frac{r_r}{T_{max} \times \eta_{T(1st)} \times g_a} \qquad\qquad 8.12$$

where r_r is the rolling radius, T_{max} the maximum torque from the engine, $\eta_{T(1st)}$ is the transmission efficiency (appropriate to bottom gear) and g_a the axle ratio. The weight of the vehicle (W) being the normal, or usual, weight of the vehicle.

First gear ratio fixed in this manner has been found to be adequate. Indeed, one cannot do better in terms of gradeability and acceleration from rest. The method has been checked for a wide range of vehicles from the low powered to the racing car and produces a sensible bottom gear ratio in every case.

Having looked at techniques for fixing top and bottom gear ratios we now turn to the intermediate gear ratios. The first question to answer is "How many do we need?" The answer is "sufficient to provide adequate 'overlap' between the gear ratios." By overlap we mean that the engine is not taken through its effective speed range during a gear change. It has some range in reserve. This means that towards either end of the engine speed range the vehicle will operate satisfactorily in one of several gear ratios. If little or no overlap is provided the vehicle is very tiresome to drive in hilly terrain. An engine speed limit is reached demanding a gear change which, when made, has to be returned to the former ratio because the terrain has changed. The amount of overlap required should be such that the vehicle speed range appropriate to a particular gear encroaches upon that of its neighbours, above and below, by some 20-25 %.

The adequacy may be determined by the conduction of a time-to-speed calculation and a comparison with the results of such calculations assuming a different number of gear ratios. Figure 8.2 shows the percentage difference in the calculated time-to-speed of a small 1 litre car equipped with a five speed and a three speed gearbox when compared with its normal four speed gearbox. Clearly, the three speed gearbox is not adequate and the five-speed gearbox shows a small improvement only. The four speed gearbox is the sensible choice.

Having fixed the number of intermediate gear ratios, we now have to give them suitable values. It is as well first to look at the simple and, seemingly, logical philosophy which would set the ratios in geometric progression. This is illustrated in Figure 8.3 in which the engine is shown to operate through a particular speed range having limits N_{e_u} and N_{e_l}. These, of course, are not the absolute upper and lower limits of the engine speed but are designed to provide adequate overlap. The relationship between engine speed and vehicle speed for a particular gear ratio is a straight line through zero. As the line for first gear reaches the upper limit of engine speed a gear change is necessary to alter the engine speed to its lower limit. This then determines the slope and hence the value of the second gear ratio. Proceeding in this manner it may be shown that the resulting gear ratios are in geometric progression.

Now, this technique may be adequate for fixing the intermediate gear ratios of a heavy commercial vehicle. Indeed, there is some merit in this if a two speed axle is to be employed since the set of ratios with one axle ratio can be made to be interposed between that of the other axle ratio, without duplication of overall gear ratios or anomalous ratios.

However, a cursory glance at the specifications contained in the brochures of manufacturers will show that the gear ratios of motor

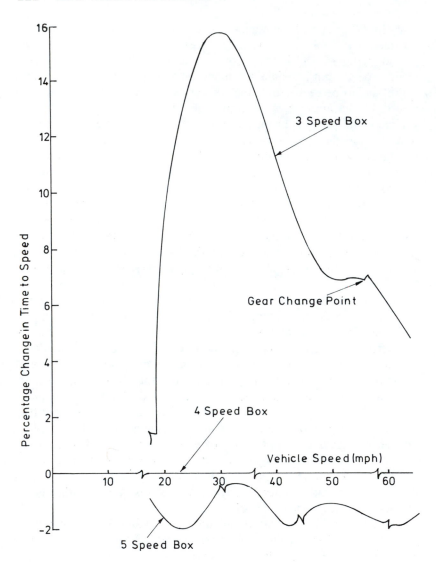

FIGURE 8.2   Number of gear ratios

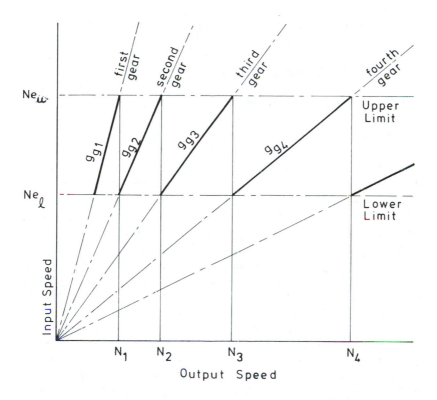

FIGURE 8.3   Intermediate gear ratios (geometric progression)

cars are not arranged in geometric progression. In fact, it is nearer the truth to say that the vehicle speed range is constant for each of the speed ratios. In practice the intermediate gear ratios are geared higher (lower numerical value) than if they were geometric progression. This provides less overlap in the lower gears and more in the higher gears.

The reason for this leads us to a better understanding of the purpose of the intermediate gear ratios. They are not simply to take the vehicle from the bottom to top gear regime. Ratios set in geometric progression will achieve this. Rather they are to achieve this with the greatest alacrity. This, then, suggests a suitable technique for the fixing of the intermediate gear ratios of a motor car, that they should be such that the time-to-speed to the beginning of the top gear speed regime should be a minimum.

Before looking at this more carefully it must be stressed once again that, normally, intermediate gear ratios are not fixed by the conscious use of any such technique. Their values are fixed from the experience embodied in the Designer. The human brain, armed with experience, is very good at juggling with a set of values to achieve an optimum result. This can be much simpler than the use of an elaborate mathematical technique to achieve the same end.

However, we do not all possess this experience. Further, with the use of computer programs for vehicle performance predictions with the suggestion that the range of vehicle specifications may be considerably wider than common practice, the reliance upon experience could be a hindrance. In these circumstances, it is preferable to build into such programs the ability of the program to fix the gear ratios most suitable for the particular vehicle specification.

Now there are optimisation subroutines in the libraries of most computer centres and one of the direct search techniques would be applicable here. These employ a subroutine of our own writing which generates the value of a function, in this case the time for the vehicle to reach a particular speed. The independent variables are juggled in a systematic manner appropriate to the technique in order that the value of the function may be a minimum (or a maximum, if desired). For our work, the variables are the intermediate gear ratios. Had we made the mistake of writing our original time-to-speed subroutine (Chapter 5) with the gear change as specified values, rather than dependent variables, we would have had to include these also in the list of variables.

A number of such direct search techniques are satisfactory for this work. Two worthy of mention are the Rosenbrock technique* and the Powell technique**. The former has the facility for the specification of constraints; say, that a gear ratio cannot be negative, or that third gear ratio must lie between second and fourth. It homes rapidly to the vicinity of the optimum but thereafter tends to take a relatively long time to make real progress. The latter technique is excellent at homing onto the optimum when quite near, the usual situation in the

---

*Rosenbrock, H.H. "An automatic method for finding the greatest or least value of a function". The Computer Journal, Vol 3, 1960, pp. 175-184.
**Powell, M.J.D. "An efficient method for finding the minimum of a function of several variables without calculating derivatives". The Computer Journal, Vol 7, 1964, pp. 155-162.

choice of intermediate gear ratios. We would expect our initial guess to be quite near. An obvious initial guess would be to put the reciprocals of the gear ratios in arithmetic progression. The Powell technique can be made to work to constraints by, say, optimising on the square of the variables to prevent their going negative and by the use of cosine functions to keep them between particular limits. The use of such pseudo-constraints in a technique which does not naturally include constraints is very desirable in work such as fixing the intermediate gear ratios. There is no sense in allowing an expensive machine to churn away only to tell you that to your specified bottom and top gear ratios of 4.118 and 1.000 it has selected second and third gears to be −468.346 and +1036,782, even though, by some quirk, they may in theory result in a lower time-to-speed than any other set. Both the Rosenbrock and the Powell (with pseudo-constraints) techniques have been found to work well for this task.

For those of us without access to standard optimisation library subroutines, the job can be done very well, very quickly and using little computer store by programming a simple "shakedown" routine. This makes use of the observation that the function to be optimised, the time to a particular speed, is a very well behaved function when plotted against one of the variables; an intermediate gear ratio. It progresses smoothly in value down through a clearly defined minimum and then rises again; there being no apparent false minima or other complications to thwart the technique. The technique takes each intermediate gear ratio in turn and searches for the minimum in the time to the specified speed. Then, because the variables are inter-related, the whole pattern of looking at each of them in turn is repeated three or four times in a sort of "shake-down" process. In mathematical circles, this would be described as a thoroughly bad technique, lacking in generality and an inelegant optimisation procedure. But, because the function is well behaved; because our initial guess is reasonably close to the optimum and because an answer to a large number of decimal places is not required anyway, from practical considerations, the method works very well, is fast, occupies little core store and is easy to program. It may be incorporated into the time-to-speed program discussed in Chapter 5.

Having sorted out a suitable optimisation technique we must now look at the answers that it gives. Table 8.1 lists the intermediate ratios as a result of optimising the time to a number of final speeds. The

TABLE 8.1
OPTIMISED INTERMEDIATE GEAR RATIOS MEDIUM SALOON CAR

gear ratio	actual ratios	0.46 mile/h	0.56 mile/h	0.66 mile/h	0.76 mile/h	0.86 mile/h
1st	3.6243	3.6243	3.6243	3.6243	3.6243	3.6243
2nd	2.1328	2.8460	2.5489	2.3515	2.0587	1.8631
3rd	1.3898	2.2926	1.9246	1.6606	1.4340	1.2576
Top	1.000	1.000	1.000	1.000	1.000	1.000

vehicle specification is that of a medium sized saloon car of 2 litre engine capacity. The actual ratios of the vehicle are given in column 2, the maximum speed of the vehicle, both measured and calculated, is 45.6 m/s (102 mile/h). Now we have intimated that, with a four speed gearbox, the final quarter of the speed range is the domain of top gear. We should look therefore at the intermediate gear ratios produced by optimising the time to three quarters of maximum vehicle speed, that is to 76 mile/h. We see from Table 8.1 that the gear ratios produced are not identical to the actual ratios, but are close. Sufficiently close in fact to constitute a workable set.

This technique has been tried over a wide range of motor cars and has been found to produce a reasonable set of intermediate gear ratios. In the absence of design experience in this field therefore, the technique is a rational alternative.

9 Hydrokinetic Transmissions

A transmission component, frequently associated with the conventional automatic transmission system, is the hydrokinetic, or, as it is sometimes called, the hydrodynamic device. This consists of essentially the transmission of power by the high velocity of fluid (oil) between the rotating elements of a pump and a turbine. While physically such units are readily distinguishable from hydrostatic units, their essential characteristic is the transference of energy by the kinetic energy of the fluid, rather than by pressure energy.

There are two main categories of hydrokinetic device; the fluid coupling which provides no torque multiplication, and the torque converter which can deliver a higher torque than it receives. The former, in its basic form, is made up of a centrifugal pump delivering oil at high velocity directly to a centripedal turbine placed adjacent to it, in the manner depicted in Fig. 9.1. The vane passages in both the pump (or impeller) and the turbine are approximately semicircular in section such that, in the assembled device, the oil is directed on a roughly circular path through the pump and turbine vane channels. The pump is driven by the engine and the turbine drives the load, both rotating about the common axis.

Since the basic fluid coupling consists of these two elements only and since, under steady-state conditions, the sum of the torques on the units must be zero, we have the condition that

$$T_1 + T_2 = 0 \qquad\qquad 9.1$$

or, that the output torque T_2 must be of the same magnitude as the input torque T_1, always. The difference in sign denotes that the output torque is of opposite direction to the input torque.

To get away from this condition in order to obtain torque multiplication, a third member must be provided. This, the reaction member, is shown situated in the fluid flow path in Fig. 9.2. Still

127

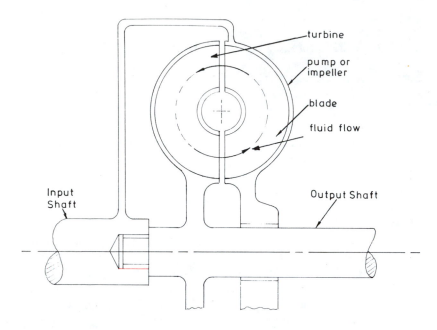

FIGURE 9.1   Fluid coupling

maintaining the essential steady-state law that the sum of torques on the complete unit must be zero, we have that, for the torque converter;

$$T_1 + T_2 + T_3 = 0 \qquad\qquad 9.2$$

from which we see that we can obtain a higher torque at output (T_2) than inlet (T_1) provided that the torque on the reaction member (T_3) is of the same sign (direction) as T_1.

The law of conservation of energy tells us that we cannot get more power out of such a unit than we put in. It follows then that, since power equals torque times rotational speed, for the output torque to be equal to or greater than the input torque, the output speed must be less than the input speed. The unit therefore must "slip" in order to function. This, and the high fluid velocity, results in the relatively low efficiency of the hydrokinetic device. Defining efficiency as output power divided by input power,

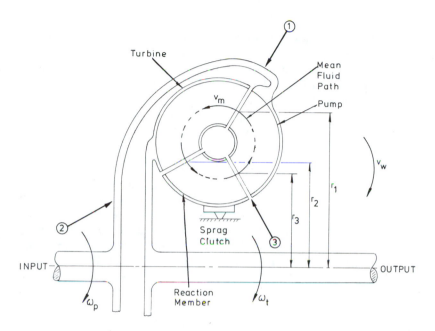

FIGURE 9.2   Torque converter

$$\eta = \frac{(-T_2) \times \omega_2}{T_1 \times \omega_1}$$

9.3

and noting that we have included the minus sign on T_2 to denote its different direction, leads us to the conclusion that, in the case of the fluid coupling in which $T_1 = -T_2$, the efficiency equals the speed ratio (ω_2/ω_1). This provides a straight line characteristic of unity slope between the efficiency and the speed ratio.

Turning now to the torque converter, if the reaction member is fixed, such that torque multiplication is possible, then as long as the output torque is higher than the input torque, the efficiency must be higher in value than that of the fluid coupling. But, if the reaction member is always fixed, we may have the torque reaction changing sign as the higher speed ratios are approached, resulting in the efficiency curve shown in Fig. 9.3, in comparison with that of the fluid coupling.

In a modern torque converter however, the reaction member is not always fixed. It is usually mounted on a sprag clutch (or free wheel device) such that when the torque reaction on this member changes sign it free-wheels. In this condition, there can be virtually no torque on the reaction member and hence the unit is, effectively, a fluid coupling having the output torque equal in magnitude to the input torque. This results in the typical torque ratio and efficiency curves shown in Fig. 9.4; the speed ratio at the point of discontinuity in slope (at which the torque on the reaction member changes sign) being called the "coupling point" of the torque converter.

Historically, the development of the torque converter started with Dr. H. Föttinger's patents, dated 1905. Units built a few years later were fitted in the drive-line of marine vessels with some measure of success. However, because of their poor efficiency at high speed ratios, their use was replaced by mechanical gearing and the fluid coupling developed by Dr. Bauer. After a steady period of development in the 1920's and 1930's, the torque converter as we know it today, having the combined functions of the original torque converter

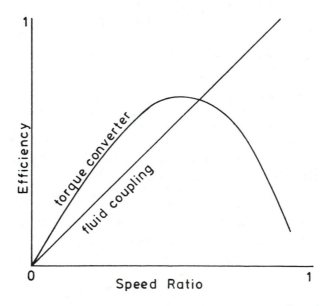

FIGURE 9.3   Fluid coupling and torque converter (fixed reaction member) efficiency

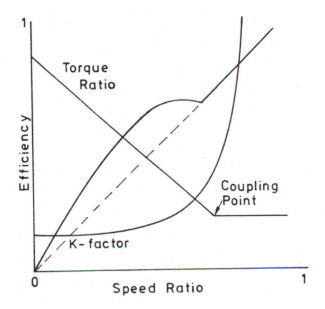

FIGURE 9.4   Torque converter characteristics

(low speed ratios) and fluid coupling (high speed ratios), came into
being. This is used in the drive-lines of the majority of American
motor cars and in the majority of European cars described as having
an automatic transmission.

A torque converter, in series with a stepped ratio automatic
gearbox, effectively constitutes another gear ratio. This is infinitely
variable in torque ratio between 1:1 at the coupling point and about
2:1 at stall. The unit is capable of smoothing out an automatic gear
change, eliminates the need for a clutch and is simple and durable. Its
main disadvantage is that, in order to function, it must slip and hence
possess a low efficiency when functioning effectively. Most automotive torque converters are designed to have a maximum torque
ratio, that is the torque ratio at stall, when the turbine is stationary, of
around the 2:1 mark. Much higher stall torque ratios can be accommodated in the basic layout shown in Fig. 9.2. Indeed the early
Föttinger converter, which used water as the fluid, had a stall torque
ratio of 5:1. But a fixed geometry design which allows a high stall
torque ratio results also in a lower maximum efficiency and a lower
coupling speed ratio.

There have been many attempts to avoid these conflicting require-ments by the use of variable geometry blade arrangements and multi-turbine and reaction member designs. These variations on the basic three element design have been reviewed by Dr. J.G. Giles in his book entitled "Automatic and Fluid transmissions" (Odhams). Further possibilities exist of including a hydrokinetic device in one path of a shunt transmission or of driving the reaction member through an epicyclic gear. These modifications to the basic layout add to the complexity and hence the cost. While they are viable, they have not been adopted generally by the very cost-conscious automotive industry. We remain with the popular arrangement of a 3-element torque converter or a 2-element fluid coupling in series with a stepped ratio gearbox.

We must now look at the performance parameters of hydrokinetic devices and the manner in which they may be used in vehicle performance calculations. In addition to the torque ratio introduced above, there need be one other only, a parameter describing the capacity of the device to accept torque. A dimensional analysis will show that the inlet torque (T_i) that a hydrokinetic device can accept is a function of pump (or impeller) speed (ω_i) and the diameter of the machine (D), viz:

$$T_i = C.\omega_i^2.D^5 \qquad\qquad 9.4$$

where C is a constant for a particular design. Traditionally this expression is re-arranged to provide a descriptor of capacity termed the K-factor and defined as

$$K = \omega_i/\sqrt{T_i} \qquad\qquad 9.5$$

Since this is a measure of the torque capacity it may seem more logical to present it as the reciprocal and perhaps squaring it, but the quotient given as expression 9.5 has become the accepted parameter. We have then, for a torque converter, two parameters necessary to define performance, the torque ratio and the K-factor. Both are functions of speed ratio and, typically, they are as presented in Fig. 9.4. The fluid coupling requires the K-factor against speed ratio curve only, the torque ratio being unity throughout the speed ratio range. The plots of efficiency against speed ratio for both the torque converter and the fluid coupling may be generated from these data (expression 9.3).

We may calculate the curves in Fig. 9.4 and show them to be functions of speed ratio by looking at the rate of change of momentum in the fluid flow at entry to and exit from each member of the hydrokinetic device. The torque converter will be used as an example here since it may be argued that the fluid coupling is only one particular form of the torque converter, having no reaction member. Fig. 9.2 depicts the juxtapositions of pump, turbine and reaction member and the mean radial distances to the gaps between members from the axial centre-line of the machine, r_1, r_2 and r_3.

The summation of the moments of the rate of change of momenta in the tangential direction at entry to and exit from a member therefore affords the net torque on the member. We require then the velocities of the fluid in the tangential, or whirl direction (v_w). This direction, and an important direction at right angles to it, namely the meridional direction, are shown in Fig. 9.2.

To obtain the velocities of whirl in terms of quantities which we know, we must view the gaps from the direction of the arrows labelled 1, 2 and 3 in Fig. 9.2 and sketch in the fluid velocity vectors. This is shown in Fig. 9.5 which defines also the blade angles at entry to (β_i) and at exit from (β_o) each member. Before setting out the relevant expressions however, we must deal with two assumptions to make matters easier. These are that the meridional flow velocity around the pump — turbine — reactor member circuit is constant, that is that the cross-sectional area normal to this velocity is constant, and that the fluid flow is one-dimensional. These enable us to consider the flow as being concentrated on a mean fluid path, shown dotted in Fig. 9.2.

We see from Fig. 9.5 that the fluid leaves the pump with an absolute velocity, or the velocity relative to the casing, (V_1) and that, having crossed gap 1, it enters the turbine with this same velocity (V_1). The velocity triangle at exit from the pump is formed from the statement that:

"The velocity relative to the casing (V_1) = the vector sum of the velocity of the fluid relative to the pump (v_{Prel})$_1$ and the velocity of the pump relative to the casing (u_{p_1})".

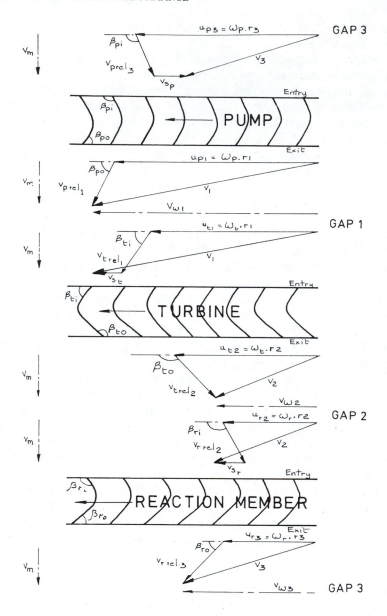

FIGURE 9.5   Torque converter velocity diagrams

This then defines the velocity triangle at exit from the pump and ensures that the arrow heads are pointing in the right direction. The triangles at exit from the turbine and the reaction member are made up in a similar manner. The absolute velocities, v_1, v_2 and v_3 may each be considered to be comprised of two components at right angles, the common meridional velocity v_m and the tangential or whirl velocities. v_{w_1}, v_{w_2} and v_{w_3} respectively.

On entering a member, unless the blade angles happen to be just right to accept the fluid cleanly, the fluid velocity triangles will not close. In general there will be a mis-match which we can represent by closing the velocity diagram with a "shock" velocity, denoted at v_{s_t}, v_{s_r} or v_{s_p} in Fig. 9.5. This, then, defines the velocity diagrams at entry to the three members.

The next task is to use these diagrams to express the important whirl, shock and relative velocities in terms of quantities we know, as far as we can. This affords the following velocity relationships.

a. whirl velocity components

$$v_{w_1} = u_{p_1} + v_m . \text{Cot } \beta_{p_o}$$

i.e. $$v_{w_1} = \omega_p . r_1 + v_m . \text{Cot } \beta_{po} \qquad 9.6$$

turbine outlet

$$v_{w_2} = \omega_t . r_2 + v_m . \text{Cot } \beta_{to} \qquad 9.7$$

reaction member outlet

$$v_{w_3} = \omega_r . r_3 + v_m . \text{Cot } \beta_{ro} \qquad 9.8$$

(note: if the reaction member is fixed, $\omega_r = 0$)

b. shock velocities

turbine inlet

$$v_{s_t} = u_{t_1} + v_m . \text{Cot } \beta_{t_i} - v_{w_1}$$

i.e. $v_{s_t} = r_1(\omega_t - \omega_p) + v_m (\operatorname{Cot} \beta_{ti} - \operatorname{Cot} \beta_{po})$ 9.9

reaction member inlet

$v_{s_r} = r_2 (\omega_r - \omega_t) + v_m (\operatorname{Cot} \beta_{ri} - \operatorname{Cot} \beta_{to})$ 9.10

pump inlet

$v_{s_p} = r_3 (\omega_p - \omega_r) + v_m (\operatorname{Cot} \beta_{pi} - \operatorname{Cot} \beta_{ro})$ 9.11

c. relative velocities

pump outlet

$(v_{p_{rel}})_1 = v_m . \operatorname{Cosec} \beta_{po}$ 9.12

turbine outlet

$(v_{t_{rel}})_2 = v_m . \operatorname{Cosec} \beta_{to}$ 9.13

reaction member outlet

$(v_{r_{rel}})_3 = v_m . \operatorname{Cosec} \beta_{ro}$ 9.14

We may now develop the torque equations by subtracting the moment of the rate of change of momentum at inlet to a member from the moment of the rate of change of momentum at exit from that member. An exception may be made in the case of the turbine since it is appreciated that the direction of the turbine torque is opposite to that of the pump. We are in order therefore in avoiding the minus sign. The torque equations are therefore:

pump torque, $T_p = \dot{m}(v_{w_1}.r_1 - v_{w_3}.r_3)$ 9.15

turbine torque, $T_t = \dot{m} (v_{w_1}.r_1 - v_{w_2}.r_2)$ 0.16

reaction member torque, $T_t = \dot{m} (v_{w_3}.r_3 - v_{w_2}.r_2)$ 9.17

From these, we obtain the power equations:

input, or pump, power $= T_p \times \omega_p$ 9.18

output, or turbine, power $= T_t \times \omega_t$ 9.19

There can be no power from the reaction member since, below the coupling point, it is fixed and hence has no angular velocity and, above the coupling point it is free-wheeling and hence can have no torque.

The torque equations, and therefore the power equations, are made up of the whirl velocities and the mass flow rate of fluid ($\dot{m}$) across the gaps. This latter quantity we have taken to be constant and may be obtained from

$$\dot{m} = \rho.v_m.A \qquad\qquad 9.20$$

where $\rho =$ the fluid density
and $A =$ the cross-sectional area of the flow path normal to the meridional velocity (v_m). The whirl velocities are already expressed in terms of quanties we know (equations 9.6 to 9.8) except for this meridional velocity (v_m). To quantify this, we have to conduct a power balance on the torque converter as a whole.

The power difference between input and output is dissipated in fluid friction and turbulence (irreversible effects) in the blade passages and associated with the shock loss velocity at entry to a member. The friction we can deal with by empirically factoring the kinetic energy of the fluid flow through the blade passages by saying

rate of friction energy loss $= \frac{1}{2}\dot{m}\,(v_{rel})^2 \times f_f$ 9.21

where $f_f =$ the friction factor and may be taken as
being in the region of 0.2 to 0.3

The nose of a blade at entry to a member may be well rounded such that the blades accept the flow reasonably cleanly over a range of conditions. In such circumstances, not all of the kinetic energy associated with the shock loss velocity may be "lost"; that is dissipated by irreversible effects. There may be some recovery. We may describe the rate of kinetic energy loss by this mechanism therefore by

$$\text{shock power loss} = \tfrac{1}{2}\dot{m}v_s^2 \times f_s \qquad\qquad 9.22$$

where $f_s =$ the shock loss factor, which may be taken as being in the range 0.8 to 1.0.

The power balance on the complete machine therefore is given by

$$\dot{m}[\omega_p(v_{w_1}.r_1 - v_{w_3}.r_3) - \omega_t(v_{w_1}.r_1 - v_{w_2}.r_2)]$$

$$= \frac{\dot{m}}{2}\,[v_{s_p}^{\,2} + v_{s_t}^{\,2} + v_{s_r}^{\,2}].f_s + \frac{\dot{m}}{2}\,[(v_{\text{Prel}})_1^2 + (v_{\text{rrel}_2}^{\,2} + (v_{\text{rrel}})_3^2]f_f \qquad 9.23$$

since these fluid velocities may be expressed in terms of the meridional velocity v_m, we may use equation 9.23 to find v_m. Indeed, the substitution of equations 9.6 to 9.14 into 9.23 and its re-arrangement can show that the torque ratio and the K-factor are functions of speed ratio and the geometry of the converter*. This, then may be used to predict these characteristics for a particular design of torque converter.

We now turn to the combination of these characteristics with those of the engine. The two upper graphs of Fig. 9.6 are the K-factor and torque ratio versus speed ratio characteristics of the torque converter. The lower left graph is the full throttle engine torque curve. This is modified in the lower right graph to give the engine K-factor (w_e/T_e) against engine speed. To marry together the two sets of characteristics the procedure is as follows.

1. select speed ratio (w_o/w_i) as the independent variable and divide the range into steps of 0.1. Then, for each speed ratio value

2. read off torque converter K-factor

3. since, if there is no gearing between engine and torque converter, this equals the engine K-factor, the engine speed may be read off the lower right graph in Fig. 9.6

4. enter the lower left graph with engine speed and read off engine torque

5. enter the upper right graph with the selected value of speed

---

* See Lucas, G.G. and Rayner, A. "Torque converter design Calculations" Automobile Engineer, Vol. 60, No. 2, Feb. 1970.

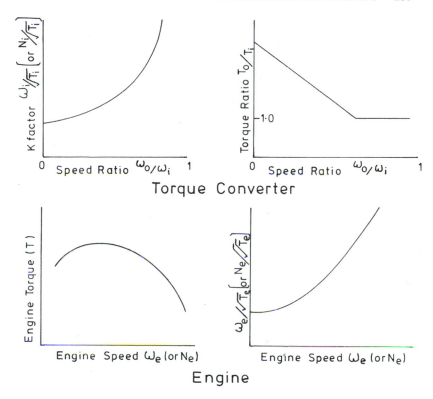

Torque Converter

Engine

FIGURE 9.6   Engine and torque converter match study (no gearing between engine
and torque converter $T_i = T_e$ and $\omega_i \, E \, \omega_e$ for steady state)

ratio and read off the torque ratio

6. multiply the torque ratio by the engine torque to give the output torque (T_o)

7. multiply the speed ratio by the engine speed to give the output shaft speed.

We now have two graphs, Fig 9.7 and 9.8 giving the output torque versus output speed and the engine speed versus output speed. The former suggests therefore that we may look upon the engine and torque converter combination as a "power unit" having an output shaft, the steady state torque characteristics of which are as depicted in Fig. 9.7. For steady-state purposes therefore, we can forget that the

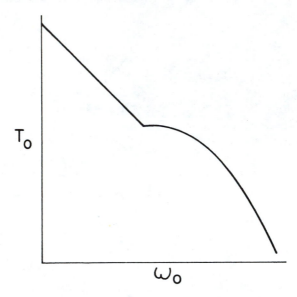

FIGURE 9.7   Torque converter output torque

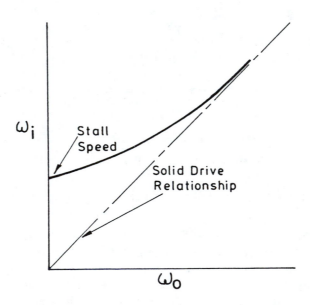

FIGURE 9.8   Enginee speed vs torque converter output speed

unit consists of two major components married together.

Having married the two, we must study the match to see if it is desirable. Experience has taught us that the engine speed at stall should be around the 2000 rev/min mark for the medium sized car. Too high and the coupling between engine and output shaft is too loose, resulting in a "fussy" engine with a marked change in engine speed with each change in load. Too low and the coupling is too tight, resulting in creep at idle, that annoying feature of having to keep the brake hard on to prevent the car moving forward at traffic lights. A further feature to be deprecated in a match is a dip in the engine speed versus output speed curve (Fig. 9.8). This curve should rise steadily from the stall value to the maximum engine speed. It would be disconcerting to the driver if, on accelerating away from rest, he could sense his engine speed dropping before rising later.

The propensity of vehicles having a fluid coupling to creep at idle is sometimes dealt with by the provision of a "well" in the fluid circuit. The low speed of the pump at idle results in the fluid falling into the well rather than being flung out to the periphery of the fluid circuit. This effectively breaks the fluid coupling. Another frequent appendage to the fluid coupling is a centrifugal clutch affixed to the pump casing which locks the pump and turbine together at high engine speed, thereby preventing slip and so increasing the efficiency of the coupling to unity.

We now have a well matched power unit, consisting of an engine and torque converter or fluid coupling, having an output shaft of known characteristics (Fig. 9.7). It might be supposed therefore that we could now continue to conduct vehicle performance calculations in the manner outlined in Chapter 5. We can, but there is one major proviso which we shall deal with in Chapter 10.

In the meantime the reader may care to try his hand at the following calculations as a means of familiarising himself with torque converter performance.

1. A three element torque converter has a flow area of $0.00795\,m^2$ and contains a fluid of density $820\,kg/m^3$. The radius of the gap between pump and turbine is $0.0984\,m$, between reactor and pump is $0.0564\,m$ and between turbines and reactor is $0.0564\,m$. The blade angles at exit from the pump, turbine and reaction member are $97°$, $112°$ and $22°$.

If the input shaft speed is 300 rad/s, the speed of the output shaft 150 rad/s and the meridional velocity of the fluid is 8.06 m/s calculate the whirl velocities of the fluid at exit from the pump, turbine and reaction member. The speed ratio is below the coupling point.

Hence calculate the input torque, the output torque and the efficiency of the torque converter.

(28.5 m/s, 5.2 m/s, 19.95 m/s, 88.4 Nm, 132 Nm, 75 %).

2. If the blade angles at entry to the pump, turbine and reaction member of the torque converter described in question 1 are 95°, 55° and 90° respectively, calculate the magnitudes of the shock velocities at entry to pump, turbine and reaction member.

(3.735 m/s, 8.127 m/s, 5.204 m/s).

3. Determine the velocities of the fluid relative to the moving member at exit from the pump, turbine and reaction member for the torque converter described in question 1. If the shock loss factor is taken as unity, calculate the friction factor.

8.12 m/s, 8.69 m/s, 21.52 m/s, 0.25).

4. If the output speed of the torque converter in question 1 is altered to 285 rad/s to give a speed ratio higher than the coupling point, calculate the speed of rotation of the reaction member and the efficiency of the machine. Take the new meridional velocity of the fluid to be 2.61 m/s.

(152 rad/s, 95 %).

10 Performance of Automatics

By far the greatest number of transmission systems described as "automatic" consist of a torque converter in series with a stepped ratio epicyclic gearbox in the manner depicted in Fig. 10.1. In other respects the transmission system is similar to a manual. In the U.S.A., the norm in motor car transmissions is the automatic; the manual transmission being the exception. Also, automatic transmissions are employed quite extensively in the heavy commercial vehicle field. In Europe and Asia their use is not nearly so widespread being confined mainly to the larger luxury class of motor car and some commercial vehicles.

The introduction of the torque converter into the system, such that the speed of the engine and of the vehicle are not tied rigidly together, makes it desirable to study the performance of the automatic transmissioned vehicle separately from that of manuals. The conventional system layout (Fig. 10.1) is of an engine, torque converter, stepped ratio automatic epicyclic gear box and then to the axle and drive wheels. The use of an epicyclic gearbox enables power to be transmitted during a gear change. This feature of epicyclics, covered later in Chapter 11, is able to be exploited because there is no clutch in series with the main drive line.

The gear ratio changes are made by operating brake bands and clutches within the automatic gearbox, usually by hydraulic means. The engine therefore is arranged to drive a hydraulic pump in order to power the operation of these clutches and work the control system. Some automatic gearboxes incorporate a second pump, the rear pump, driven from the output shaft. This is arranged to be capable of serving the hydraulic system independently of the front pump, or engine driven pump, during, say, a push or tow start. In recent years however, the tendency has been to omit this rear pump on the grounds of cost rendering the vehicle incapable of being started by a tow.

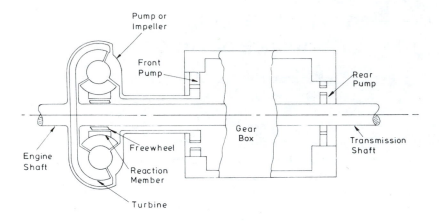

FIGURE 10.1   Typical automatic transmission layout

The automatic differs also from the manual in that the gear change speeds are pre-specified. The hydraulic control system accepts speed and load signals and automatically changes gear at pre-set conditions. These gear change points therefore must be specified before the start of time-to-speed calculations.

Our problem therefore is as shown in Fig. 10.2 of two subsystems connected by the torque converter. The left hand side subsystem consists of an engine delivering torque against an accelerating inertia and a restraining torque (T_i) imposed by the torque converter. This latter torque, as we saw in Chapter 9, is a function of the speed ratio across the torque converter, that is of engine speed and the speed of the other subsystem, the vehicle subsystem. In this the torque delivered by the torque converter (T_o) accelerates the vehicle against an opposing load imposed by the drag of the vehicle. In Fig. 10.2, all inertia and torques in the vehicle subsystem are related to the linear motion of the vehicle itself.

Conventionally, therefore, one could write down the equations of motion for the two subsystems, as follows; for the accelerating engine

$$T_e - T_i = I_e \cdot \frac{d\omega_e}{dt} \qquad\qquad 10.1$$

and for the accelerating vehicle,

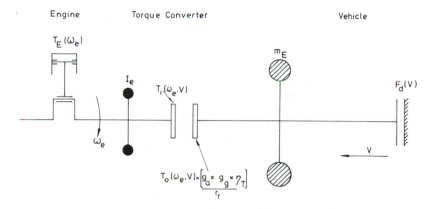

FIGURE 10.2   Mathematical model of automatic transmission

$$(T_o \times \frac{g_a \times g_g}{r_r} \times \eta_T) - F_d = M_E \cdot \frac{dv}{dt} \qquad 10.2$$

where the output torque from the torque converter is given by

$$T_o = T_i \times TR \qquad 10.3$$

and TR is the torque ratio of the torque converter.

Equations 10.1 and 10.2 are two differential equations having time, t, as the independent variable and dependent variables, ω_e and V. In vehicle performance calculations however, it is more convenient to consider the vehicle speed, V, as the independent variable, if only because the gear change points with an automatic transmission are at predetermined speeds. Therefore, putting together equations 10.1 and 10.2 and rearranging yields:

$$\frac{d\omega_e}{dV} = \frac{T_e - T_i}{Ie} \times \frac{M_E}{[T_o \times ((g_a \times g_g)/r_r) \times \eta_T] - F_d} \qquad 10.4$$

Equations 10.4 and 10.2 may now be solved using a standard numerical technique to yield the engine speed at a particular vehicle speed and the time-to-speed during an acceleration run. A suitable numerical technique would be the Runge–Kutta process, or one of its variations. These exist as standard algorithms in any computer library.

The integration process may be started by setting the engine acceleration ($d\omega_e/dt$) to zero since, on a time-to-time speed test, the driver is usually instructed to depress both the throttle and brake pedals and to lift his foot off the brake pedal at $t = 0$. However, the handling of the gear changes in the integration process presents a difficulty. Strictly, one should specify in detail the gear change process itself, enabling one to make the integration process continuous throughout the gear change. This entails specifying full details of the clutches and inertias within the gear box and their behaviour; a cumbersome proposition since these data may not be known in detail. A simpler technique is to assume zero engine acceleration after a gear change and to start again from this new boundary condition. Although this condition is not true in practice, its assumption here may be justified because the time involved is so small compared with the overall time of an acceleration run.

Even so the programing may seem formidable to the reader compared with that of the manual transmission and certainly the computer time involved in running such a program is considerably greater than that for the manual program. This is important because such vehicle performance programs are frequently used in parametric studies in which a particular design parameter is successively altered and its effect noted. This multiplies the computer time by the number of parametric values considered. A further objection to tackling the writing of such a program by the use of an integration package is that it becomes difficult to interrupt the process to deal with such contingencies as wheel-spin.

There are better ways of dealing with this problem. If we refer back to Chapter 9 we see that the match between the engine and torque converter results in a characteristic of the steady-state output torque against the torque converter output shaft speed. We can write our time-to-speed program therefore in much the same way as that for the manual transmission by substituting this torque characteristic for the engine torque. This is simple and obvious, but there is one important snag. The vehicle, and the engine, are accelerating, and so the operation of the torque converter is not as the steady state condition. While it is permissible to assume quasi-steady-state operation of the torque converter, that is to say we may assume that it sticks to its characteristic graphs of torque ratio and K-factor during an acceleration, the output torque will be less than the steady state because the input torque is less by the amount needed to accelerate the engine. This drop in input torque to the torque converter upsets the match and results in a lower output torque than the steady-state. We should therefore cater for this in our computer program.

To calculate the drop in engine torque in dealing with its own inertia we need to know the engine acceleration. This is related in some way to the vehicle acceleration, the quantity we are attempting to find. One method therefore would be to guess the engine acceleration and to work through the performance calculations to give the vehicle acceleration. This may then be used to check the guessed value which may be successively modified until it corresponds. Such an iterative process is a little clumsy, but workable. It is not a desirable technique however because we are still probing about unnecessarily in the innards of the torque converter.

The choice of torque converter has a small influence only on vehicle time-to-speed such that it is chosen for a particular application primarily from other considerations. These are described in Chapter 9 and concern the need for a particular engine stall speed and a rising engine speed characteristic; conditions relating to the engine and torque converter alone and which do not concern the rest of the vehicle. It would be desirable therefore to avoid the need to read in torque converter characteristics in order to perform vehicle time-to-speed calculations. We would like to be able to use the steady state torque curve direct and not have to repeat the match study between engine and torque converter every time. This is possible if we can describe the match between engine and torque converter mathematically and so predict the change in output torque of the unit under dynamic conditions.

Out mathematical description of Chapter 9 is a little too heavy to deal with what is, after all, a second order point. It is apposite therefore to see what happens to the engine–torque converter steady-state match study when the level of engine torque is reduced by a small amount. Fig. 10.3 shows the effect on engine speed and Fig. 10.4 the effect on torque converter output torque. The lower curve in both figures is the result of repeating the match study with the engine torque reduced by a fixed amount, of the same order expected from an accelerating engine. These show that, in accelerating the engine's

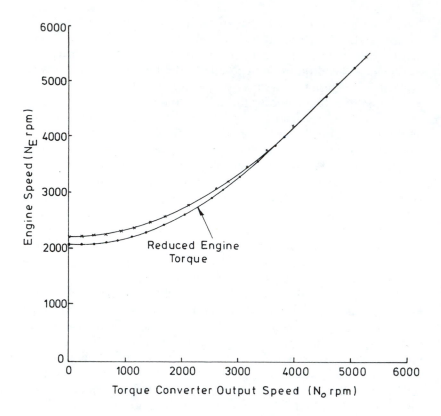

FIGURE 10.3   Engine speed — T.C. output speed, effect of engine torque level

own inertia, a match point moves down and to the left.

The amount it moves may be deduced as follows:

Let the engine torque drop by a small proportion, a, in accelerating its own inertia. Then, the torque delivered is

$$T_{e_I} = T_{e_{I=0}} \times (1 - a) \qquad\qquad 10.5$$

where $T_{e_{I=0}}$ is the steady rate, or zero inertia torque from the engine.

Two sets of relationships may be obtained from the torque converter. These are

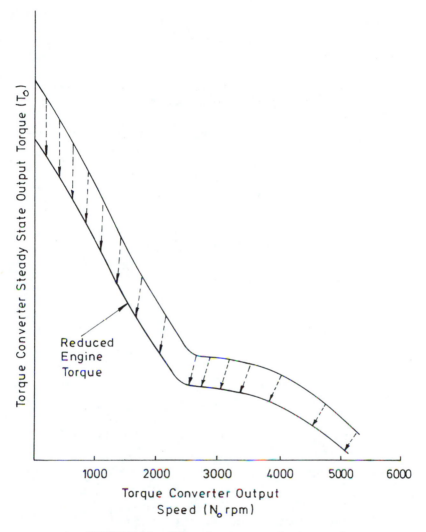

FIGURE 10.4   Effect of engine torque level on match

$$T_{o_{I=0}} = TR \times T_{e_{I=0}} \qquad\qquad 10.6$$

$$T_{o_I} = TR \times T_{e_I} \qquad\qquad 10.7$$

and

$$N_{o_{I=0}} = SR \times N_{e_{I=0}} \qquad\qquad 10.8$$

$$N_{o_I} = SR \times N_{e_I} \qquad\qquad 10.9$$

where T_o (Nm) is the torque converter output torque, N_o (rev/min) the torque converter output shaft speed and N_e (rev/min) the engine speed.

If equilibrium running is assumed and we may equate the torque converter K-factor to that of the engine, we can say that

$$\frac{N_{e_{I=0}}}{\sqrt{T_{e_{I=0}}}} = \frac{N_{e_I}}{\sqrt{T_{e_I}}} \qquad\qquad 10.10$$

Using equation 10.5, this may be rewritten

$$N_{e_I} = \frac{N_{e_{I=0}}}{\sqrt{T_{e_{I=0}}}} \times \sqrt{T_{e_{I=0}}} \times (1-a)^{1/2}$$

which, on taking the first term only in a binomial expansion, because $a <<|$, becomes

$$N_{e_I} = N_{e_{I=0}} \times (1 - \frac{a}{2}) \qquad\qquad 10.11$$

Using this in conjunction with expressions 10.8 and 10.9 yields

$$N_{o_I} = N_{o_{I=0}} \times (1 - \frac{a}{2}) \qquad\qquad 10.12$$

Similarly with the torque expressions. Combining equations 10.5, 10.6 and 10.7 produces

$$T_{o_I} = T_{o_{I=0}} \times (1 - a) \qquad\qquad 10.13$$

Thus we have predicted the shift in the match point as a result of accelerating the engine.

If we define this shift in output shaft speed as

$$\Delta N_o = N_{o_{I=0}} - N_{o_I} \qquad\qquad 10.14$$

and the shift in engine speed as

$$\Delta N_e = N_{e_{I=0}} - N_e \qquad\qquad 10.15$$

and the shift in torque converter output shaft torque as

$$\Delta T_o = T_{o_{I=0}} - T_{o_I} \qquad\qquad 10.16$$

we may write, with the aid of expressions 10.12 and 10.13, that

$$\frac{\Delta N_o}{N_{o_{I=0}}} = \frac{\Delta N_e}{N_{e_{I=0}}} = \frac{\Delta T_e}{2T_{e_{I=0}}} = \frac{\Delta T_{o_I}}{2T_{o_{I=0}}} \qquad\qquad 10.17$$

This, therefore, enables us to use the steady-state torque output from the torque converter since we can predict the change resulting from the accelerating engine.

To do this let us look at enlarged details of Figs. 10.3 and 10.4 in Figs. 10.5 and 10.6. A study of the Fig. 10.6 shows that if the accelerating vehicle is, at a particular instant, at speed V corresponding to a torque converter output speed of $N_{o_{I=0}}$. The steady-state torque output is given by point A; however, since a real engine has inertia, point C on the lower curve is applicable, whereas the expression derived above (10.17) enables us to know the torque output at point B. We may say therefore that the torque output we require is given by

$$T_{o_C} = T_{o_A} - \Delta T_{o_I} - \Delta T_{o_m} \qquad\qquad 10.18$$

where T_{o_A} is the steady state torque, ΔT_{o_I} is the change due to engine inertia and ΔT_{o_m} is the change in torque due to the mis-match (or the shift sideways of the operating point).

Fig. 10.6 shows the latter term to be given by

$$\Delta T_{o_m} = -\left(\frac{\delta T_o}{\delta N_o}\right)_B \times \Delta N_o \qquad\qquad 10.19$$

where suffix B refers to point B in Fig. 10.6.

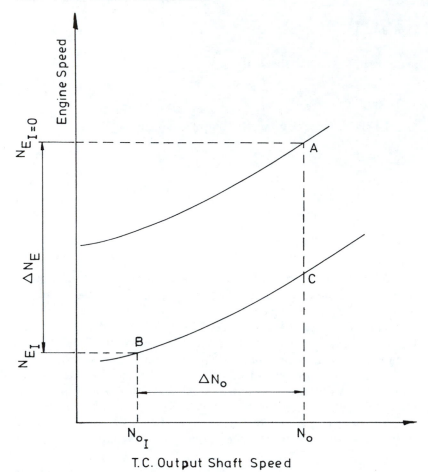

FIGURE 10.5   Effect of accelerating engine

Using equation 10.17 and noting that

$$(\delta T_o/\delta N_o)_A \simeq (\delta T_o/\delta N_o)_B \qquad\qquad 10.20$$

results in the change in torque due to mismatch

$$\Delta T_{om} \simeq -(\frac{\delta T_o}{\delta N_o A}) \times N_{0_{I=0}} \times \frac{\Delta T_{o_I}}{2T_{o_{I=0}}} \qquad\qquad 10.21$$

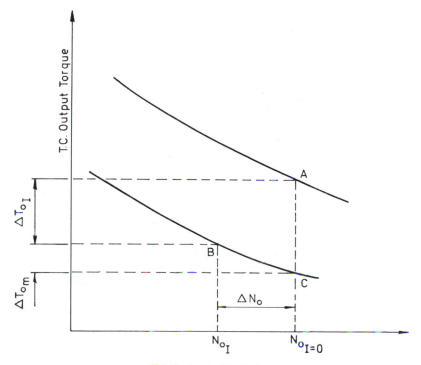

FIGURE 10.6   Change in match due to accelerating engine

To obtain the other change in output torque (ΔT_{o_I}) we must find first the engine inertia torque. This is given by

$$\Delta T_e = I_e \times \frac{\delta N_e}{\delta t} \times \frac{2\pi}{60} \qquad\qquad 10.22$$

which, by using the relationship between the angular acceleration of the torque converter output shaft and the acceleration of the vehicle (f)

$$\frac{\delta N_o}{\delta t} = \frac{f \times g_a \times g_g}{r_r} \times \frac{60}{2\pi} \qquad\qquad 10.23$$

may be written

$$\Delta T_e = I_e \times \frac{\delta N_e}{\delta N_o} \times \frac{f \times g_a \times g_g}{r_r} \qquad \text{10.24}$$

Knowing the torque ratio (TR) of the torque converter, this may be used in conjunction with expression 10.7 to give

$$\Delta T_{o_I} = TR \times \left[I_e \times (\frac{\delta N_e}{\delta N_o}) \times \frac{f \times g_a \times g_g}{r_r} \right] \qquad \text{10.25}$$

Substituting this, first into expression 10.21 and then into 10.18 results in

$$T_{o_c} = T_{o_A} + \left[I_e \times (\frac{\delta N_e}{\delta N_o})_c \times \frac{f \times g_a \times g_g}{r_r} \left[(\frac{\delta T_o}{\delta N_o})_A \times \frac{N_o}{2T_{e_{I=0}}} - \frac{T_{o_A}}{T_{e_{I=0}}} \right] \right] \qquad \text{10.26}$$

noting also that

$$(\frac{\delta N_e}{\delta N_o})_A = (\frac{\delta N_e}{\delta N_o})_B \approx (\frac{\delta N_e}{\delta N_o})_C \qquad \text{10.27}$$

The vehicle acceleration (f) and the torque converter output torque (T_{o_c}) are linked also, by the application of Newton's second law, to the accelerating vehicle

$$f = \left[T_{o_c} \times \frac{g_a \times g_g}{r_r \times M_E} \times \eta_{T} \right] - \frac{F_d}{M_E} \qquad \text{10.28}$$

These two expressions may be combined to give the formidable looking expression

$$T_{o_c} = \frac{\dfrac{T_{o_A}}{[T_{o_A} - (\delta T_o/\delta N_o)(N_o/2)]} \cdot \dfrac{T_{e_{I=0}}}{[I_e \times (\delta N_e/\delta N_o)]} + \left[(F_d/M_E)\dfrac{g_a \times g_g}{r_r}\right]}{\dfrac{\eta_T}{M_E}\left\{\dfrac{g_a \times g_g}{r_r}\right\}^2 + \dfrac{T_{e_{I=0}}}{[T_{o_A} - (\delta T_o/\delta N_o)(N_o/2)]} \cdot \dfrac{1}{I_e \times (\delta N_e/\delta N_o)}}$$

10.29

Formidable it may look, but all the terms on the right hand side are known or are immediately calculable. The torque converter output shaft speed N_o is the independent variable and T_{o_A} is the torque converter steady state output torque obtained from the match study with the engine. The differential expressions $(\delta T_o/\delta N_o)$ and $(\delta N_e/\delta N_o)$ may be readily obtained by expressing the results of the engine–torque converter match study by polynominals.

$$T_o = a_o + \sum_{j=1}^{n} a_j (N_o)^j \qquad\qquad 10.30$$

and

$$N_e = b_o + \sum_{i=1}^{m} b_i (N_o)^i \qquad\qquad 10.31$$

An eighth order ($n = 8$) being adequate, usually, to describe the former and a sixth ($m = 6$) the latter. A feature of the polynominal expression being the ease with which it may be differentiated.

The fitting of polynominal expressions to the results of a match study between the engine and the torque converter, a once only exercise which, if carried out using a digital computer, can be arranged to afford the match in terms of polynominals, enables the output torque to be evaluated in a straight-forward manner, without iteration. Vehicle performance calculations may then be calculated in the manner outlined in Chapter 5 using T_{o_c} in place of the engine torque.

This technique of evaluating the performance of automatic transmission vehicles is outlined in more detail and compared with that using a proprietory mathematical technique (Runge–Kutta) in the Proceedings of the Institution of Mechanical Engineers, Automotive

Division, Drive Line 70. 1970. It has been found to be an accurate, quick and reliable method, well suited to parametric studies.

The error in taking the steady-state torque converter output characteristics and ignoring the foregoing is significant and may be assessed by conducting a vehicle performance calculation using the above and then repeating with the engine inertia (I_e) set at zero. The result of such a study is illustrated in Fig. 10.7 for a medium-sized saloon car and shows an error of some $7^1/2\%$ in the time-to-speed calculation at about the first gear change speed.

The procedure therefore for the calculation of the time to speed of an automatic transmission vehicle should be to first conduct a match study between engine and torque converter and to use the output of this to evaluate the time-to-speed in a manner similar to that outlined for manual transmissions in Chapter 5. If a digital computer is to be used to conduct the match study, it may be programmed as follows:

1. fit a sixth-order polynominal to the engine net torque curve

2. from this, express engine speed as a sixth-order polynomial function of the steady-state engine K-factor.

3. read-in 20 to 30 torque converter speed ratio values and their corresponding K-factor and torque ratio figures

4. for each torque converter speed ratio value, set the engine K-factor equal to the torque converter K-factor and evaluate the steady-state engine speed using the sixth-order polynomial in (2) above.

5. from this engine speed, evaluate the engine torque at each speed ratio point using the polynomial in (1) above.

6. hence, for each speed ratio point, evaluate the torque converter output torque from the product (engine torque × torque ratio), and the output shaft speed from the product (engine speed × speed ratio).

7. fit an eighth-order polynomial to the torque converter output torque against output speed figures.

8. fit a sixth-order polynomial to the engine speed against output shaft speed data.

This describes the match between engine and torque converter

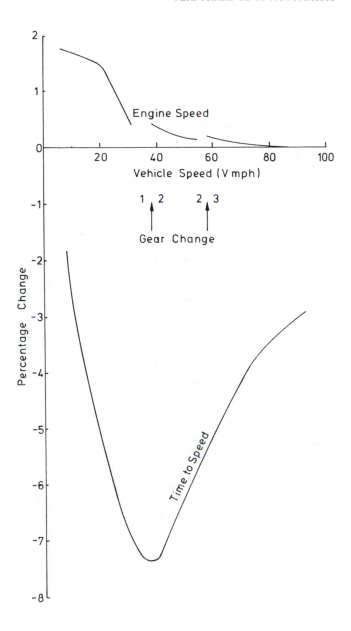

FIGURE 10.7   Error in assuming $i_e = 0$

and, if satisfactory, we may proceed to evaluate the time-to-speed as follows:

Split the vehicle speed range, V_1 to V_2, into about 25 to 50 equal step lengths, ΔV, and for each one, evaluate;

a. the dynamic rolling radius, r_{r_v} (expression 4.28)

b. the drag force, F_d (expression 4.8)

c. the gear ratio currently engaged from a knowledge of the gear change speeds

d. the overall gear ratio, $G = 2\pi/60 \times \dfrac{r_{r_v}}{g_g \cdot g_a}$ m/s per rev/min of engine speed.

e. the transmission efficiency, η_T

f. the equivalent mass of the vehicle, M_E (expression 4.5)

g. the torque converter output shaft speed, $N_o = V/G$ rev/min

h. the steady-state torque converter output torque using the eighth order polynomial expression from the match study

i. the first differential of this torque with respect to the output speed, $\delta T_o/\delta N_o$

j. the net output torque by subtracting the torque necessary to drive the rear hydraulic pump, if fitted, from the steady-state torque converter output torque

k. the engine speed using the sixth order polynomial expression from the match study

l. the first differential of the engine speed with respect to the output speed, $\delta N_e/\delta N_o$

m. the engine torque from knowledge of the engine speed. Subtract the torque necessary to drive the front hydraulic pump in the gearbox

n. the torque converter output torque allowing for the effect of the accelerating engine from expression 10.29

o. the tractive force at the wheels, $F_t = T_o \times \dfrac{g_g \times g_a}{r_{r_v}} \times \eta_T$

p. the propulsive force, $F_p = F_t - F_d$

q. and, hence, the vehicle acceleration $f = F_p/M_E$

The time-to-speed may be integrated between the two speed limits in precisely the manner outlined in Chapter 5 for manual transmissions.

The calculation of the steady-state fuel consumption also follows the pattern for manual transmission vehicles as set out in Chapter 6. The only difference is that the torque converter output torque and power are used in place of the engine torque and power. This may be determined from a number of match studies between engine and torque converter at different throttle angle settings, or it may be achieved by placing the engine and torque converter together on a test bed and proceeding in the manner described earlier for the engine alone.

11   Epicyclic Gear Trains

The basic epicyclic gear train, consisting of a central sun wheel around which planet wheels may rotate, in conjunction with the enclosing annulus gear, as shown in Fig. 11.1, is, at first sight at least, very attractive for automotive purposes. The terms "sun" and "planet" almost certainly stem from the use of the epicycle in the Ptolemaic system of the universe as an attempt by ancient Greek philosophers to describe the motion of heavenly bodies.

In the epicyclic gear train the centre of the planet (or planets, since it is usual to provide two or more equally spaced planets for reasons of balance and load sharing) is capable of rotating about the main centreline. The shaft of the planet therefore is carried in bearings by a "carrier", and this constitutes the third power path of the epicyclic gear train, or differential gear as it is sometimes called. The other two power paths being via the sun gear and the annulus gear. By using two of these shafts for the input and output of power and by

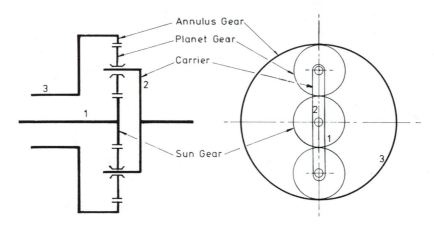

FIGURE 11.1   Epicyclic gear

160

controlling the speed of the third member, a versatile transmission unit results. The speed ratio across the unit may be varied by altering the speed of the third member. It follows therefore that it is possible to alter the speed ratio of the transmission without disruption of power flow. It is not necessary therefore to close down the engine during a gear change.

The relationship between the speeds of the three shafts may be derived by first considering one shaft, say the carrier (shaft 2 in Fig. 11.1), to be fixed. We then have a simple train of gears all having fixed centres and a speed ratio given by

$$R_{13} = \frac{\omega'_3}{\omega'_1} \qquad\qquad 11.1$$

where ω'_3 and ω'_1 are the speeds of shafts 3 and 1 when shaft 2 is fixed. The basic ratio R_{13} is given by the number of teeth on the sun wheel with respect to the number of teeth on the annulus gear. Thus

$$R_{13} = \frac{-t_1}{t_3} \qquad\qquad 11.2$$

The minus sign denoting that the sun and annulus rotate in opposite directions when the carrier is fixed.

But, in an epicyclic gear train, the carrier is not necessarily fixed; it too may be rotating at, say, a speed ω_2. We can consider this by taking our simple train with the fixed carrier and rotating the whole (sun, carrier and annulus) at speed ω_2. In this way the speed of the sun now becomes

$$\omega_1 = \omega'_1 + \omega_2 \qquad\qquad 11.3$$

and that the annulus

$$\omega_3 = \omega'_3 + \omega_2 \qquad\qquad 11.4$$

but the basic relationship described by expression 11.1 is unchanged. It is as though we had mounted our simple train onto a board and then rotated the board at speed ω_2 thereby giving the carrier a speed

ω_2 and superimposing this speed onto that of the sun and of the annulus. Our basic relationship can now be written as

$$R_{13} = \frac{-t_1}{t_3} = \frac{\omega_3 - \omega_2}{\omega_1 - \omega_2} \qquad\qquad 11.5$$

which, upon rearrangement, becomes

$$\omega_3 = R_{13}\,\omega_1 + (1 - R_{13})\omega_2 \qquad\qquad 11.6$$

In deriving this relationship linking the speeds of the three shafts we need not have considered the carrier to be fixed, we could have obtained a basic ratio R_{23} with, say, shaft 1 fixed and obtained the relationship

$$\omega_3 = R_{23}\omega_2 + (1 - R_{23})\omega_1 \qquad\qquad 11.7$$

From which we see that

$$R_{23} = 1 - R_{13} \qquad\qquad 11.8$$

This exercise could be repeated to show also that the basic ratio with shaft 3 fixed, R_{12}, is given by

$$R_{12} = \frac{R_{13}}{R_{13}-1} \qquad\qquad 11.9$$

If we know one basic ratio therefore, we can write down the values of the other two and so describe any epicyclic gear in the manner shown by Fig. 11.2. The rectangle denotes the epicyclic gear train, which need not be a simple train, it could be compounded. It is described by one basic ratio, in this case R_{13}, and the three shafts are numbered 1, 2 and 3. Using this notation it is, of course, immaterial that shaft 1 be connected to a sun. It could be connected to a carrier or an annulus. For performance purposes therefore, we need not concern ourselves with the hardware inside the epicyclic gear-box provided that we know one of the basic ratios.

In addition to the three basic ratios already mentioned there are

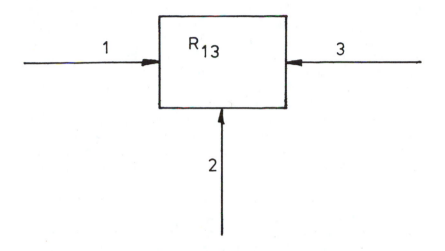

FIGURE 11.2   Systems description of an epicyclic gear

three others, but these, R_{31}, R_{32} and R_{21} are the reciprocals of R_{13}, R_{23} and R_{12} respectively.

We have seen that a fixed speed relationship exists between two shafts of a differential unit if we can dictate the speed of the third shaft. This may be achieved by fixing it with a brake such that its speed is zero, clutching it to either the input or the output shaft or by driving it from the input or the output through another epicyclic gear, that is by compounding. Consider a simple train, Fig. 11.1, in which the number of teeth on the annulus gear is twice the number on the sun. The basic ratio R_{13} therefore is -0.5. By fixing the annulus ($\omega_3 = 0$) we have, from equation 11.6, that

$$\omega_2 = \frac{R_{13}}{R_{13}-1}\,\omega_1 = \frac{-0.5}{-1.5}\,\omega_1 = \frac{1}{3}\,\omega_1 \qquad 11.10$$

Fastening the annulus to either the input or the output shaft results, again from equation 11.6, in

$$\omega_2 = \omega_1 = \omega_3 \qquad 11.11$$

that is that the epicyclic is locked out of action and everything is rotating at the one speed. By driving the annulus gear at some speed intermediate between 0 and ω_1 through another similar epicyclic train we can obtain a speed ratio between $1/3$ and 1. This can be arranged in the manner shown in Fig. 11.3 and so provides a useful three-speed gearbox. Fixing the annulus of the main train gives bottom gear, in this case $1/3$ or, in common parlance, 3 to 1 reduction. Releasing the annulus of the main train and fixing that of the subsidiary train affords intermediate gear, while releasing both annulii and engaging the clutch provides 1 to 1, or top gear ratio. If the subsidiary train also has twice the number of teeth on the annulus as on the sun then the resulting intermediate gear ratio may be shown to be that the output shaft speed is 5/9 times that of the input. Such an arrangement is shown schematically in Fig. 11.4 and provides the basis for the design of many of our modern automatic transmissions. One obvious advantage being that as one brake or clutch is being released and another is being engaged in a gear ratio change, power is still being transmitted through the transmission giving what has become to be termed, a "hot-shift". No control is necessary therefore to close the engine throttle. Other advantages, of lower bearing and tooth loads, stem from the universal practice of providing two or more planet wheels in each train.

A physical constraint is that, since the teeth on the sun, the planets

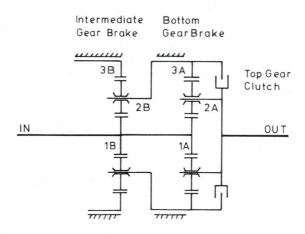

FIGURE 11.3   Compound epicyclic gear

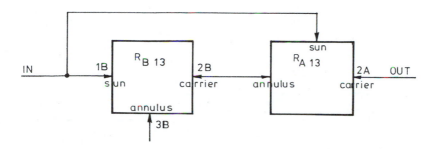

FIGURE 11.4   Schematic arrangement of compound epicyclic gear

and the annulus must all be of the same diametral pitch, that is the same size, the sum of the number of teeth on the sun and twice the number of teeth on a planet wheel must equal the number of teeth on the annulus. Further, if n equally spaced planets are employed, in order that they may be assembled, the sum of the numbers of teeth on the sun and the annulus, when divided by n, must afford an integer.

An example of compounding to provide four forward gear ratios and one reverse is shown in the Wilson gearbox layout in Fig. 11.5. Operating brake b_1 on the annulus gear a_1 of the main train, or set 1, provides bottom gear. Releasing this and holding the annulus a_2 of the second set with brake b_2 gives second gear. Engagement of brake b_3 instead of b_2, which fixes the sun s_3 of the third train provides third gear. While the release of all brakes and the engagement of the clutch locks up the system to give a 1 to 1 top gear ratio. Reverse gear is obtained by the engagement of brake b_r only. If the numbers of teeth on the suns s_1, s_2, s_3 and s_r are 23, 23, 20 and 31 respectively, while those on the annulii a_1, a_2, a_3 and a_r are 67, 67, 58 and 65 respectively, the reader is encouraged to verify that the ratios provided are 0.2556, 0.4458, 0.6817, 1.0 and −0.1958.

Equation 11.6 tells us that we can express the speed of one shaft relative to another provided that we know the speed of the third. A more fundamental property of the three shaft differential, or epicyclic gear system, is that it splits torque. We need to quote the torque in one shaft only and the torque levels in the other two shafts are then known irrespective of the speeds of the shafts. If the differential is of perfect mechanical efficiency and the torque in shaft 1 is T_1 then the torque in shaft 2 is $-T_1/R_{23}$, or $T_2 = -((R_{13}-1)/R_{13}).T_1$, and $T_3 =$

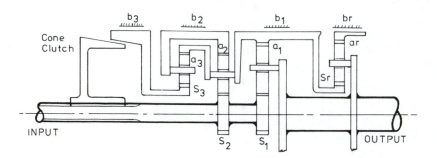

FIGURE 11.5   Wilson gearbox

$-T_1/R_{13}$. That this must be so may be adduced from equilibrium considerations. The negative signs ensure that the direction of the torques in shafts 2 and 3 are described correctly relative to that of shaft 1. The analogous linear differential is shown as Fig. 11.6 in which the rods 1, 2 and 3 have velocities V_1, V_2 and V_3 which are related to each other in some way by the ratio a/b. Two velocities must be specified in order to obtain the third. However, irrespective of the velocities, the force in rod 3 must be that in rod 2 factored by the ratio a/b and $F_2 + F_3 = F_1$ if the system is in equilibrium and free of friction.

The torque sign convention leads to the power sign convention that power flows are positive into the system. In the case shown in Fig. 11.7(a) in which the input power P_1 is split two ways along shafts 2 and 3, P_2 and P_3 must be considered as being negative. Fig. 11.7(b) shows two power flows P_1 and P_2 converging to give one output power P_3. In this case P_3 is negative.

We now turn to the practical consideration that real gear trains do not transmit power without loss. Considering the case depicted by Fig. 11.7(a) in which a differential feeds power from shaft 1 to shafts 2 and 3. We may modify the torque split relationships given above to

$$T_2 = \frac{-E_{12}.T_1}{R_{23}} = \frac{-E_{12}}{R_{13}}\frac{(R_{13}-1)}{}T_1 \qquad\qquad 11.12$$

$$\text{and } T_3 = \frac{-E_{13}\,T_1}{R_{13}} \qquad\qquad 11.13$$

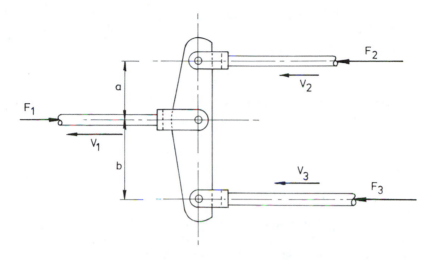

FIGURE 11.6   Linear differential gear

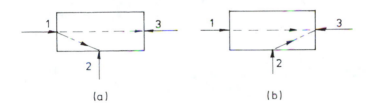

(a)   (b)

FIGURE 11.7   Power sign convention

The efficiency factors, E_{12} and E_{13}, therefore modify the output torques and as such must be related. The relationship may be obtained by noting that the sum of the torques on the system, with imperfect efficiencies, must still equal zero to maintain equilibrium. That is that

$$T_1 + T_2 + T_3 = 0 \qquad\qquad 11.14$$

or that $T_1 - \dfrac{E_{12}\,(R_{13}-1)}{R_{13}} - \dfrac{E_{13}}{R_{13}}\,T_1 = 0$ \qquad\qquad 11.15

Isolating E_{12} results in the relationship that

$$E_{12} = \frac{R_{13} - E_{13}}{R_{13} - 1} \qquad\qquad 11.16$$

which suggests that if $E_{13} = 1$; $E_{12} = 1$ also.

From relationship 11.16 in conjunction with equations 11.12 and 11.13 therefore we may say that

$$T_3 = \frac{-E_{13}T_1}{R_{13}} = \frac{E_{13}}{R_{13} - E_{13}} T_2 \qquad\qquad 11.17$$

is true for any real epicyclic gear box. It is necessary therefore to specify the efficiency factor of one power flow path, together with one basic ratio, when describing a real three shaft differential.

The sum of the powers entering an imperfect differential will not equal zero since irreversibilities in the system must result in a power loss in the form of a rate of energy conversion to heat. The power equation may be obtained by multiplying expression 11.17 by the input speed (ω_1) to give

$$T_3 . \omega_3 . \frac{\omega_1}{\omega_3} = \frac{-E_{13}}{R_{13}} . T_1 \, \omega_1 = \frac{E_{13}}{R_{13} - E_{13}} \, T_2 . \omega_2 . \frac{\omega_1}{\omega_2}$$

or that

$$P_3 . \frac{\omega_1}{\omega_3} = \frac{-E_{13}}{R_{13}} P_1 = \frac{E_{13}}{R_{13} - E_{13}} P_2 \frac{\omega_1}{\omega_2} \qquad\qquad 11.18$$

It is left to the reader to show that equations 11.17 and 11.18, the torque and power equations, result in this same form if the power flow system of Fig. 11.7(b) is considered. In doing this, it will be realised that

$$E_{23} = \frac{E_{13} (1 - R_{13})}{E_{13} - R_{13}} \qquad\qquad 11.19$$

The efficiency factors E_{13} and E_{23} are, of course, connected and both are related to the efficiency of the epicyclic. The expression for the efficiency of the epicyclic depends upon which of the two flow patterns shown in Fig. 11.7 is used. If there is one input power flow and two output power flows, Fig. 11.7(a), the efficiency is defined as

$$\eta = \frac{-P_2 - P_3}{P_1} \qquad 11.20$$

The minus signs are used to conform to the power flow convention of positive into a unit.

Using the power split expression, 11.18 in conjunction with the speed expression of an epicyclic, 11.6, enables equation 11.20 to be rearranged as follows

$$\eta = \frac{E_{13} - R_{13}}{R_{13}(R_{13} - 1)} \left[\frac{\omega_3}{\omega_1} - R_{13} \right] + \frac{E_{13}}{R_{13}} \cdot \frac{\omega_3}{\omega_1} \qquad 11.21$$

This gives the relationship between the efficiency, η, as the efficiency factor, E_{13}.

For the other power flow condition, depicted in Fig. 11.7(b), of two input power flows and one output power flow, the efficiency is defined as

$$\eta = \frac{-P_3}{P_1 + P_2} \qquad 11.22$$

Again, using the power split expression, 11.18, in conjunction with the speed split expression, 11.6, results in the relationship

$$\eta = \frac{E_{13} \cdot (1 - R_{13}) \, \omega_3 / \omega_1}{R_{13}(1 - R_{13}) + (E_{13} - R_{13}) \cdot (\omega_3 / \omega_1 - R_{13})} \qquad 11.23$$

The efficiency, η, will be less than or equal to unity. However, the efficiency factor, E_{13}, may be greater than unity.

Further information on the derivation and the connection between these terms may be obtained from Lucas, G.G., "Expressions governing the power flow through differential mechanisms having imperfect efficiencies" Proc. I. Mech. E. C12/84 Driveline 84.

Before turning to performance calculations on vehicles employing epicyclic gear trains in Chapter 12, it is as well to consolidate the work of this chapter by a worked example as follows:

"Calculate the torque transmitted by, and the power flow in the component parts of the Wilson gearbox depicted in Fig. 11.5 when operated in third gear. The input speed is 200 rad/s and the input torque is 500 Nm (ie input power = 100kw). Take the efficiency factors of the main epicyclic set, with the power flow from sun to carrier, as 0.96 and that of the second set, sun to carrier, as 0.98, while that of the third set, annulus to carrier, as 0.97.

Hence determine the overall efficiency".

Fig. 11.8 shows, in systematic form, the gearbox in third gear. Power enters on line 1 and leaves on line 0. Power enters the main set through lines 8 and 9. Power enters the second set on lines 2 and 3 and leaves on line 4. The power flow through the third epicyclic set is from line 5 to 7, line 6 being fixed to the casing. While it is not immediately apparent that the power flow directions are as described, the following calculations confirm that this is so. For convenience, Fig. 11.8 shows the relevant components marked s=sun, a=annulus or c=carrier.

The first step is to determine the basic ratios of the three epicyclic sets.

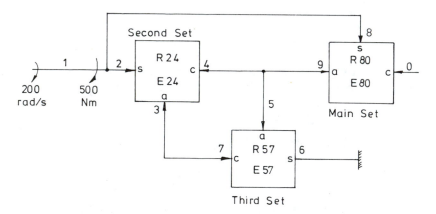

FIGURE 11.8   Schematic of Wilson gearbox in third gear

Set 1; $R_{89} = \dfrac{-23}{67} = -0.3433$, $R_{80} = \dfrac{R_{89}}{R_{89}-1} = \dfrac{-0.3433}{-0.3433-1} = 0.2556$

Set 2; $R_{23} = \dfrac{-23}{67} = -0.3433$, $R_{24} = \dfrac{R_{23}}{R_{23}-1} = \dfrac{-0.3433}{-0.3433-1} = 0.2556$

Set 3; $R_{56} = \dfrac{-58}{20} = -2.9$, $R_{57} = \dfrac{R_{56}}{R_{56}-1} = \dfrac{-2.9}{-3.9} = 0.7436$

Torque

Dealing first with Set 2.

$$T_3 = \dfrac{-(R_{24}-E_{24})}{R_{24}} T_2 \text{ (see equation 11.17)}$$

ie $T_3 = \dfrac{(-0.2556 - 0.98)}{0.2556} T_2 = 2.834. T_2$

and $T_4 = \dfrac{-E_{24}}{R_{24}}.T_2 = \dfrac{-0.98}{0.2556}. T_2 = -3.834.T_2$

(note that $T_2 + T_3 + T_4 = 0$)

turning now to Set 3.

$T_7 = -T_3 = -2.834. T_2$

$T_5 = \dfrac{-R_{57}}{E_{57}} T_7 = \dfrac{-0.7436 \times -2.834.T_2}{0.97} = 2.173\ T_2$

$T_6 = \dfrac{(R_{57} - E_{57})}{R_{57}} T_5 = \dfrac{-(0.7436 - 0.97) \times 2.173.T_2}{0.7436} = 0.6616.\ T_2$

we can now look at Set 1.

$$T_9 = -T_4 - T_5 = (3.834 - 2.173)T_2 = 1.661.T_2$$

$$T_8 = \frac{R_{80}}{-(R_{80} - E_{80})} \, T_9 = \frac{0.2556}{-(0.2556 - 0.96)} \times 1.661.T_2 = 0.6027.T_2$$

$$T_0 = \frac{-E_{80}}{R_{80}} . \, T_8 = \frac{-0.96}{0.2556} \times 0.6027.T_2 = -2.264.T_2$$

but $T_2 + T_8 = 1.6027T_2$ equals the input torque 500Nm

giving $T_2 = 312.0$Nm and the other torque levels therefore are as given in table 11.1.

Using the speed relation (expression 11.6) the speed of the various components, as given in table 11.1, may be verified.

The product (torque and speed) affords the power into a set, a negative sign denoting that power is flowing out of the relevant epicyclic set.

$$\text{The overall efficiency, } \eta_{10} = \frac{-P_0}{P_1} = \frac{96.26}{100}. = 0.9626$$

We see from this exercise that in third gear, about one third of the input power is delivered directly to the main epicyclic set and that two thirds approximately is shunted through epicyclic sets 2 and 3, with quite a high level of power being recirculated around sets 2 and 3.

TABLE 11.1
WILSON GEARBOX, THIRD GEAR

Component		designation	angular velocity ω rad/s	torque T Nm	power P kw
input shaft		1	200.0	500	100
Set 2	sun	2	200.0	312.0	62.40
	annulus	3	85.13	884.1	75.26
	carrier	4	114.5	−1196.1	−137.0
Set 3	annulus	5	114.5	677.8	77.61
	sun	6	0	206.3	0
	carrier	7	85.13	−884.1	−75.26
Set 1	sun	8	200.0	188.0	37.60
	annulus	9	114.5	518.2	59.33
	carrier	0	136.3	−706.2	−96.26

12   Shunt Transmissions

The search for a satisfactory, infinitely variable transmission, capable of returning the fuel consumption and accelerative potentional discussed earlier in this book, has produced a number of contenders. These are primarily, the hydrostatic pump/motor combination, "frictional" devices characterised by the belt and expanding pulley and the Perbury–Hayes, hydrokinetic devices and electrical machinery. More attention is being paid to the hydrostatic and frictional devices than the others, for reasons of efficiency, size and cost.

Devices hampered by a relatively low efficiency in the rate of the transfer of energy, yet having, potentially, a wide range of ratios, such as the hydrostatic device, may be placed in a shunt system. This bypasses some power through a direct, high efficiency, mechanical drive, so raising the overall transmission efficiency. Altering the speed ratio across the variator alters the overall speed ratio and the split of power between the parallel mechanical and variator paths. Effectively, such a system trades some of the speed ratio range of the variator for a higher overall efficiency. Hydrostatic devices, with their wide ratio potential and their part load efficiency problem, are eminently suitable variators in a shunt transmission. Practical frictional devices have quite a high efficiency but do not possess a wide ratio range. A design, such as the Perbury–Hayes, Fig. 6.3, may have a ratio range of the order $-0.5 > R > -2.5$, the negative signs denoting the change in speed direction across the unit, a feature of the design. The requirement for motor vehicle propulsion is a speed ratio range of, say, -0.2 to 1.25 in conjunction with a suitable axle ratio. The former limit providing a reverse ratio and the latter some degree of overdrive. Indeed, to obtain a low fuel consumption, the 1.25 figure should increase to about 3. Clearly, therefore, a frictional device with the limits given above cannot afford to have its range reduced. The speed ratio range however for a practical hydrostatic

174

pump/motor combination may be $-3 < R < +3$; this being achieved by infinite variation of the stroke of the motor and by switching the stroke of the pump from full stroke in one direction to full stroke in the reverse direction. When the pump stroke is fixed at one of its extreme positions and the pump is run at a fixed speed, the setting of the motor stroke at its maximum will produce a low output speed. This is because the constant fluid flow rate from the pump must, neglecting the small amount of leakage across piston and port faces, be accepted by the motor. Reducing the capacity, or stroke, of the motor therefore results in an increase in its output shaft speed. The expression governing the pump/motor combination is therefore,

$$\text{fluid flow rate} = D_p.\omega_p = D_m.\omega_m \qquad\qquad 12.1$$

where w_p is the rotational speed of the pump and w_m that of the motor. D_p is the displacement per revolution of the pump, fixed at a positive or a negative value depending on the direction of rotation. It is convenient to put a negative sign on D_p when w_p is negative. D_m is the displacement per revolution of the motor and is infinitely variable between, say, zero and its maximum value. It, too, may be positive or negative. Expression 12.1, therefore, is used to describe the control of the hydrostatic transmission.

Placing a hydrostatic pump/motor in a shunt in order to bypass some of the power involves the use of a differential. Now any variator is itself a differential or three shaft machine. The three shafts being, for a hydrostatic pump/motor unit, the pump shaft, the casing of the pump and the motor and the motor shaft. These are labelled 1, 2 and 3 respectively in Fig. 12.1 which depicts therefore the simplest of shunt transmission systems; the "Casing" shunt transmission. In this differential, the basic ratio is variable and is given by

$$R_{13} = \omega_m/\omega_p \text{ when the casing is fixed and the motor shaft is free}$$

$$\text{i.e. } R_{13} = D_p/D_m \qquad\qquad 12.2$$

Using the speed equation for a three shaft differential we have that

$$\omega_3 = 0 = R_{13}\,\omega_1 + (1-R_{13})\omega_2$$

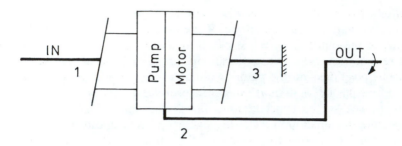

FIGURE 12.1   'Casing' shunt transmission

or

$$\omega_o/\omega_i = \frac{-R_{13}}{1-R_{13}} = \frac{1}{1-D_m/D_p}$$ 12.3

from which we see that ω_o/ω_i is always positive if D_p/D_m is arranged to be negative. This may be achieved by fixing the pump stroke at maximum and varying the motor stroke between zero and full stroke in the opposite sense such that, with the casing fixed and the motor shaft free, the motor rotates in the opposite direction to the pump.

When the motor stroke is set at zero the motor can accept no fluid from the pump; there can be no relative rotational speed therefore between the pump shaft and the casing, i.e. $\omega_2 = \omega_1$, giving a speed ratio of unity.

As the motor stroke is increased from zero the casing speed (output speed) falls below the input speed to provide the condition that the fluid flow rate produced by the pump running at a relative speed of $(\omega_1-\omega_2)$ is matched to the motor running at its relative speed of $(\omega_3-\omega_2)$.

Since $\omega_3=0$, we have that

$$(\omega_1-\omega_2)D_p = (0-\omega_2)D_m$$ 12.4

which is identical to expression 12.3.

The lowest speed ratio is obtained by setting the motor stroke at its greatest value and it approaches zero as the motor stroke approaches infinity.

In order to conduct vehicle performance calculations we require to know the output speed. We may then proceed in the manner laid down in chapters 5 and 10. The torque ratio across the transmission is less than the reciprocal of the speed ratio due to the power loss in the hydraulic leg of the shunt. Therefore, we require the power entering this hydraulic leg and the efficiency of its transfer.

The efficiency of a hydrostatic pump/motor combination decreases as the output (motor) speed is increased and as the power transmitted decreases. If the relationship for a particular unit is not know, the following expression may be used:

$$\eta_H = 0.9 - \frac{0.6|\omega_m|}{1000} - 0.2\,\frac{(P_{H_{max}} - P_H)}{P_{H_{max}}} \qquad\qquad 12.5$$

where ω_m (rad/s) is the modulus of the relative speed of the motor, P_H is the power transmitted hydraulically and $P_{H_{max}}$ the maximum power capability of the hydraulic leg. This expression has been fitted to experimental data from a typical hydrostatic pump/motor combination for a constant speed of the pump in the middle of its speed range.

If the torque input to the casing shunt transmission is T_1, the input power is $P_1 = T_1\omega_1$. We see, therefore, that the power entering the hydraulic leg is

$$P_H = T_1\,(\omega_1 - \omega_2) \qquad\qquad h12.6$$

that is the product of the input torque and the relative rotational speed of the pump. The power loss from the hydrostatic conversion is

$$P_L = P_H\,(1 - \eta_H) \qquad\qquad h12.7$$

and the overall efficiency of the transmission is

$$\eta_o = \frac{P_1 - P_H(1 - \eta_H)}{P_1}$$

or, when expression 12.6 is substituted for P_H

$$\eta_o = 1 - \frac{(1-\omega_2)}{\omega_1}(1-\eta_H) \qquad\qquad 12.8$$

This shows the overall efficiency to increase as the speed ratio ω_2/ω_1 increases, a worthwhile feature. The proportion of the power entering the hydraulic leg of the shunt increases linearly as the speed ratio is reduced (expression 12.6) such that when a low ratio is demanded in order to accelerate from a low speed or to scale a gradient, the proportion of the power subject to the hydraulic conversion is high. In the cruise and high speed regime in which the speed ratio approaches unity, the proportion of hydraulic power is low and the overall efficiency high.

The performance of this transmission is best illustrated by a worked example: Determine the speed ratio, the overall efficiency and the hydraulic power characteristics of a casing shunt transmission having a hydrostatic displacement ratio range $0 > D_m/D_p \geqslant -3$.

Take the hydrostatic efficiency to be that given by expression 12.5 and the input speed to be 100 rad/s.

By setting out the range of D_m/D_p in column 1 of Table 12.1 we may use expression 12.3 to give the overall speed ratio in column 2. The proportion of power in the hydraulic leg, column 3, is given by expression 12.6 and the hydraulic efficiency η_H, column 5, is given by expression 12.5. Expression 12.8 may then be used to give the overall efficiency in column 6.

From this we see that the mitigating condition of a high power flow through the hydrostatic unit maintaining a moderately high level of

TABLE 12.1
PERFORMANCE OF A CASING SHUNT TRANSMISSION

D_m/D_p	Speed Ratio ω_o/ω_i	$P_H/P_i = 1-\omega_o/\omega_i$	Motor Relative Speed ω_m rad/s	η_H	η_O
0	1.0	0	100.0	0.64	1.00
−0.5	0.6667	0.3333	66.67	0.73	0.91
−1.0	0.5	0.5	50.00	0.77	0.89
−1.5	0.4	0.6	40.00	0.80	0.88
−2.0	0.3333	0.6667	33.33	0.81	0.87
−2.5	0.2857	0.7143	28.57	0.83	0.88
−3.0	0.25	0.75	25.00	0.84	0.88

hydraulic efficiency which increases as the speed ratio decreases results in a fall off in the overall efficiency of unity at a speed ratio of unity to a near constant value of 0.88 at the lower speed ratios. Had we assumed a constant value throughout for the hydraulic efficiency we would have seen the overall efficiency continue to drop as the speed ratio decreased. The overall efficiency values in column 6 correspond to the maintenance of full power at inlet. Running the transmission at under-capacity with a lower inlet power level results in lower overall efficiency figures.

Table 12.1 shows the effective overall speed ratio range to be 0.25 to 1.0. A slipping device, such as a clutch, therefore is required to enable the vehicle to be moved from rest; the transmission not being infinitely variable through zero speed ratio. Alternatively, an arrangement must be made to reduce the pump stroke to zero.

The overall efficiency of the transmission may be increased still further by incorporating a mechanical differential unit in the manner shown in Fig. 12.2. This enhancement however, is again at the expense of a further reduction in the speed ratio range. Such a system may be depicted schematically, as in Fig. 12.3, and recognised as one of the two fundamental forms of single differential shunt transmission systems. This may be described as an output coupled system because the two parallel power flow paths are coupled at their output ends. The other type, the input coupled single differential shunt transmission system, is depicted in Fig. 12.4 and has distinctly different characteristics.

Let us deal first with the output coupled system. The incoming power is split by the differential along a high efficiency mechanical path and through a variator (hydrostatic) device. The two power

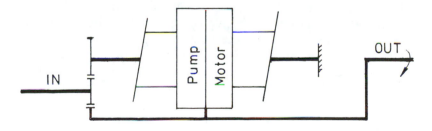

FIGURE 12.2   Differential with casing transmission

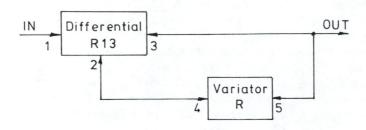

FIGURE 12.3   Output coupled single differential shunt transmission

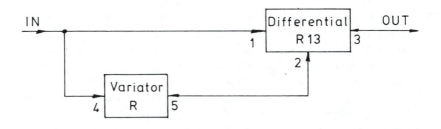

FIGURE 12.4   Input coupled single differential shunt transmission

flows are then rejoined at the output shaft. If the design of the pump and motor allows a concentric drive, physically, the transmission may be arranged in the manner depicted in Fig. 12.5.

Our development of the single differential shunt transmission from the casing shunt transmission by the additional of a differential gear does not mean that we have to keep the variator in the form depicted in Fig. 12.1. Indeed, it is more logical to fix the casings of the pump and motor and take the hydraulic leg of the drive through the pump shaft, the hydraulic connections between pump and motor and out on the motor shaft. This alters the characteristics of the variator, but this can be compensated for by altering the basic ratio of the main differential.

The differential splits to torque into the two paths in a fixed ratio,

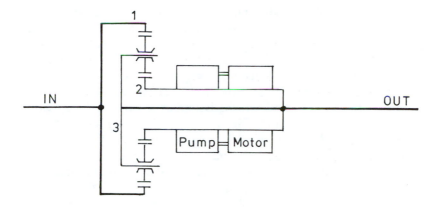

FIGURE 12.5   Layout of single differential shunt transmission (output coupled)

depending on its basic ratio. Since the speeds of the two links alter as the overall ratio is changed, the power flows into the two links vary. This may be arranged to provide a low power flow through the hydrostatic link, and hence a higher overall efficiency, during an often used part of the speed ratio regime, say the cruise condition.

The speed split follows from the speed equation of the differential unit, which is, using the nomenclature of Fig. 12.3,

$$\omega_3 = R_{13}\omega_1 + (1-R_{13})\omega_2 \qquad\qquad 12.9$$

Noting that ω_3 is the output speed ω_0, that ω_1 is the input speed ω_i and that ω_2 is given by

$$\omega_2 = \omega_4 = \frac{\omega_0}{R}$$

where $R = \omega_5/\omega_2$ is the ratio of the variator, gives the overall speed ratio as

$$\omega_o/\omega_i = \frac{R_{13}.R}{R+R_{13}-1} \qquad\qquad 12.10$$

The basic ratio R_{13} of the differential is fixed by the design. The variator ratio R is altered in order to obtain the desired overall speed ratio. We see immediately, from expression 12.10, that when R=0, obtainable by setting the hydrostatic pump stroke to zero, the overall speed ratio is zero. Hence, we may drive the vehicle in a progressive manner in the forward direction from rest without the need of a slipping clutch in the transmission system by progressingly increasing the pump stroke. At some point in the speed ratio range, when the pump is on full stroke, we may proceed further by progressively reducing the motor stroke from full to zero.

The power split along the two legs of the shunt transmission is given by expression 11.18 in chapter 11. The use of this is best illustrated by a worked example.

"A hydrostatic pump and motor are arranged in an output coupled, single differential shunt transmission in the manner shown in Fig. 12.5. The ratio of the number of teeth on the annulus gear to that on the sun is 3. The mechanical efficiency of the differential may be taken to be unity. Calculate, for a speed ratio of the hydrostatic variator of −0.05,

a) the speed ratio of the transmission

b) the proportion of power delivered to the hydrostatic line

c) the overall efficiency of the transmission for the particular part load condition when the efficiency of the hydrostatic variator is 21.0%"

Basic ratio, R_{12}=−3,

$$\text{Basic ratio } R_{13} = \frac{R_{12}}{R_{12}-1} = \tfrac{3}{4}$$

whence, from expression 12.10, the overall speed ratio,

$$\frac{\omega_o}{\omega_i} = \frac{0.75 \times (-0.05)}{(-0.05) + 0.75 - 1} = 1.125 \text{ ANS.(a)}$$

the speed of the input to the variator is given by expression 12.9, viz

$$\omega_2/\omega_1 = \frac{\left(\dfrac{\omega_o - R_{13}}{\omega_1}\right)}{1 - R_{13}} = \frac{0.125 - 0.75}{1 - 0.75} = -2.5$$

The power entering the hydrostatic leg is given by expression 11.18,

$$P_4 = -P_2 = \frac{(R_{13} - E_{12})}{R_{13}} \frac{\omega_2 \cdot P_1}{\omega_1} = \frac{(0.75 - 1)}{0.75} \times (-2.5).P_1$$

$$P_4 = 0.8\dot{3}.P_1 \quad \text{ANS.(b)}$$

the power loss from the variator is, therefore, $P_4 \times (1 - 0.21) = 0.6583.P_1$ and, since this is the only source of power loss, the overall efficiency of the transmission is

$$\eta = (1 - 0.6583) = 34.1\dot{6} \ \% \ \text{ANS (c)}$$

This worked example serves to show that the use of a shunt can, indeed, increase the efficiency of the transmission above that which would exist by employing the hydrostatic variator alone.

It is left to the reader to evaluate the power flow and overall efficiency throughout the speed range of the transmission.

For a practical output coupled single differential shunt transmission, if the pump and motor are arranged to rotate in the same direction for forward speed, the basic ratio, R_{13}, of the differential should be 1.5 approximately. Alternatively if the pump and motor are arranged to rotate in opposite directions, the basic ratio, R_{13}, should be 0.75 approximately.

The other configuration of the single differential shunt, the input coupled (Fig. 12.4), has characteristics which are not normally considered suitable for use in a transmission. For instance, with normal power flows, without recirculation, the power flow through the variator increases with increase in the overall speed ratio. Hence the overall efficiency decreases as vehicle speed increases. Yet, there are two viable systems which employ an input coupled, single differential shunt.

One, the Sunstrand DMT, depicted schematically in Fig. 12.6, employs two clutches, annotated A and B. During the low speed and

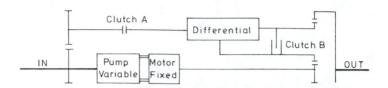

FIGURE 12.6   Schematic of Sunstrand DMT transmission

reverse regime, clutch A is free and clutch B is engaged, the latter locking up the differential. The drive now is a straightforward hydrostatic drive and not a shunt. From full reverse to 20% forward speed and the pump stroke is varied from maximum in reverse through neutral to maximum in the forward direction. The capacity of the motor is fixed at all times.

At 20% forward speed the speeds of the input and output of clutch A are the same. It is an easy matter therefore to arrange the automatic engagement of clutch A and the simultaneous disengagement of clutch B. We now have an input coupled single differential shunt transmission. The pump stroke is progressively moved back from the fully forward to the maximum in reverse as the vehicle speed is increased from 20% to 100% of its maximum speed. In the speed regime just above 20%, there is some power recirculation within the system. A full description of the transmission is given by Ross, W.A. "Designing a hydromechanical transmission for heavy duty trucks", SAE paper No. 720725, 1972.

The other employs the Perbury–Hayes system as the variator within an input coupled single differential shunt transmission. The Perbury–Hayes by itself, has a high efficiency, but a low speed ratio range. B.L. Technology Ltd., have shown considerable ingenuity in the design of the transmission shown in Fig. 12.7, which effectively increases the ratio range of this type of unit. Let us consider first the low speed and reverse range. Here, clutch A is disengaged and brake B is applied. Moving the discs within the Perbury–Hayes unit from one extreme position to the other, alters the overall ratio from reverse to low forward speed in a progressive manner. Approximately in the middle of this range is a "geared" neutral condition. That is that the drive shaft out of the transmission has zero speed but that there is no disconnection of the drive. When brake B is engaged and clutch A is

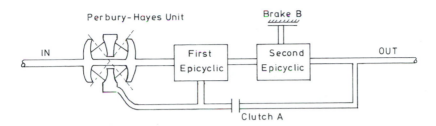

FIGURE 12.7   BL technology shunt transmission

free the transmission is an input coupled, single differential shunt system.

At the extreme position of the low forward speed regime the speeds of the two members of clutch A are equal. Again, as with the Sunstrand DMT, it is relatively easy therefore to arrange for the automatic engagement of clutch A and the simultaneous disengagement of brake B. This puts the second epicyclic gear set out of action and hence no power flows through it. The transmission now becomes a continuously variable transmission using, effectively, the Perbury–Hayes unit alone. Moving the discs within the unit from the extreme position at which clutch A is engaged back to the other extreme progressively increases the output speed to the full speed.

Again, as with the Sunstrand DMT, there is power recirculation within the transmission during part of the shunt regime. This causes a lower efficiency than would otherwise result. For further details of the BL Technology transmission the reader is referred to Stubbs, P.W.R. "Development of a Perbury Traction Transmission for Motor Car Applications" ASME paper No. 80-C2/DET-59.

Further gains in efficiency may be made by employing a continuous variable device, such as the hydrostatic pump and motor, in a shunt system having two differential gears. Such a transmission, devised by The Motor Industry's Research Association, is shown in Fig. 12.8. Here, two mechanical and one hydrostatic power flow paths exist. Again, however, the further increase in the overall efficiency of the system is made at the expense of the ratio range.

The overall speed ratio of the system is readily calculable if the basic ratios of the two differentials are known. Using the nomenclature of Fig. 12.8, since basic ratios R_{23} and R_{45} are obtained

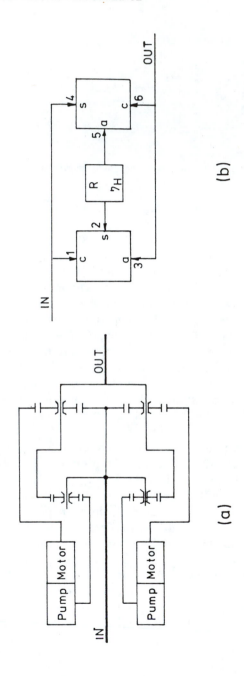

FIGURE 12.8   Double differential shunt transmission

directly from the numbers of teeth on the suns and annulii respectively, we shall derive the overall speed ratio in terms of these.

From the speed equations of the two differentials, we have that:

$$\omega_3 = R_{23}.\omega_2 + (1-R_{23}).\omega_1 \qquad\qquad 12.11$$

$$\text{and } \omega_5 = R_{45}.\omega_4 + (1-R_{45}).\omega_6 \qquad\qquad 12.12$$

now, $\omega_1 = \omega_4 = \omega_i$ and $\omega_3 = \omega_6 = \omega_0$

also, $\omega_5 = R.\omega_2$, where R is the variator ratio

putting these equalities into equations 12.11 and 12.12 and re-arranging, yields;

$$\frac{\omega_0}{\omega_i} = R_{23}\frac{\omega_2}{\omega_1} + (1-R_{23}) \qquad\qquad 12.13$$

$$\text{and } \frac{\omega_0}{\omega_i} = R.\frac{\omega_2}{\omega_i}\frac{1}{(1-R_{45})} - \frac{R_{45}}{1-R_{45}} \qquad\qquad 12.14$$

Equating these two equations and isolating ω_2/ω_i, affords;

$$\omega_2/\omega_i = \frac{-R_{45} -(1-R_{23})(1-R_{45})}{R_{23}(1-R_{45}) - R} \qquad\qquad 12.15$$

putting this result back into either 12.11 or 12.12 gives the overall ratio

$$\omega_0/\omega_i = \frac{-R_{45} - \dfrac{(1-R_{23})}{R_{23}}.R}{(1-R_{45}) - \dfrac{R}{R_{23}}} \qquad\qquad 12.16$$

The overall efficiency of the transmission is defined by

$$\eta_o = -\left[\frac{P_3 + P_6}{P_1 + P_4}\right] = -\left[\frac{P_3/P_2 + \eta_H.P_6/P_5}{P_1/P_2 + \eta_H.P_4/P_5}\right] \qquad 12.17$$

The minus sign is a direct result of the sign convention for power flows (positive into a unit). We note also that the efficiency of the hydrostatic pump/motor combination is given by;

$$\eta_H = -P_5/P_2 \qquad 12.18$$

Using the power split equation for a differential (expression 11.18) in conjunction with expression 12.17, it can be shown that the overall efficiency of the double differential shunt transmission is

$$\eta_o = \frac{R.E_{13}.(E_{46}-R_{46}) - \eta_H.E_{46}.(E_{13}-R_{13})}{R.R_{13}.(E_{46}-R_{46}) - \eta_H.R_{46}.(E_{13}-R_{13})} . \omega_o/\omega_1 \qquad 12.19$$

It is left to the reader to show that the individual power flows are given by;

$$P_1 = \frac{P_{IN}.R}{\left[(\frac{R_{23}}{E_{23}-R_{23}})(\frac{\eta_H.R_{45}}{E_{45}}) + R\right]} \qquad 12.20$$

$$P_2 = \frac{R_{23}}{(E_{23}-R_{23})} . \frac{\omega_2}{\omega_1}.P_1 \qquad 12.21$$

$$P_3 = -P_1. \frac{E_{23}}{(E_{23}-R_{23})} \frac{\omega_o}{\omega_i} \qquad 12.22$$

$$P_4 = P_{IN} - P_1 \qquad 12.23$$

$$P_5 = -\eta_H. P_2 \qquad 12.24$$

and

$$P_6 = -P_4 \cdot \left(\frac{E_{45}}{-R_{45}} + 1 \right) \cdot \frac{\omega_o}{\omega_i} \qquad\qquad 12.25$$

To achieve this, start with the fact that the input power, P_{IN} = $P_1 + P_4$ and use the power split equations for both differentials.

The following example will serve to demonstrate the use of the above equations.

The detailed working is not given, but the answers to the main steps are, in the order in which they should be determined.

"A double differential shunt transmission has a tooth ratio, sun annulus, for the first (high) differential set, of 0.34 and for the second (low) set of 0.415.

For a speed ratio of the hydrostatic variator, $R = \omega_5/\omega_2 = 0.3$, at which speed ratio the efficiency of the variator is 74%, determine the overall speed ratio, the power flows and the overall efficiency. Take the efficiency factors of the two differentials to be unity."

$$R_{23} = -0.34, \ R_{13} = 1 - R_{23} = 1.34$$

$$R_{45} = -0.415, \ R_{46} = \frac{R_{45}}{R_{45} - 1} = 0.2933$$

$$\frac{\omega_2}{\omega_1} = \frac{\omega_p}{\omega_1} = 1.896$$

$$\frac{\omega_o}{\omega_1} = 0.695$$

$$\frac{\omega_5}{\omega_1} = \frac{\omega_2}{\omega_1} \times R = 0.569 \ \left(= \frac{\omega_m}{\omega_1} \right)$$

where ω_p and ω_m are the speeds of the pump and motor respectively.

Letting $P_{IN} = 1.000$
$P_1 = 0.794$
$P_4 = 1-0.794 = 0.206$
$P_3 = -0.412$
$P_2 = -0.382$
$P_5 = 0.283$
$P_6 = -0.489$

The minus signs denote that the flow of power is out of the respective unit.

The overall efficiency is given by either expression 12.19 or

$$\eta_o = - \left[\frac{P_3 + P_6}{P^1 + P_4} \right] = \frac{0.412 + 0.489}{1.0} = 90.1\%$$

This is a considerable increase from the efficiency which would have pertained had the variator been used alone. Fig. 12.9 however, which depicts the speeds of the pump and motor and the power flows into the shunt throughout the speed ratio range, shows that the gain in efficiency is at the expense of ratio spread and that there is no "geared" neutral unless power recirculation can be tolerated. That is that a slipping clutch device is necessary to cater for the ratio range 0 to 0.2933 in this example.

The search however continues for a shunt system which can satisfactorily increase the overall efficiency of a continuously variable transmission at an acceptable cost, noise level and efficiency.

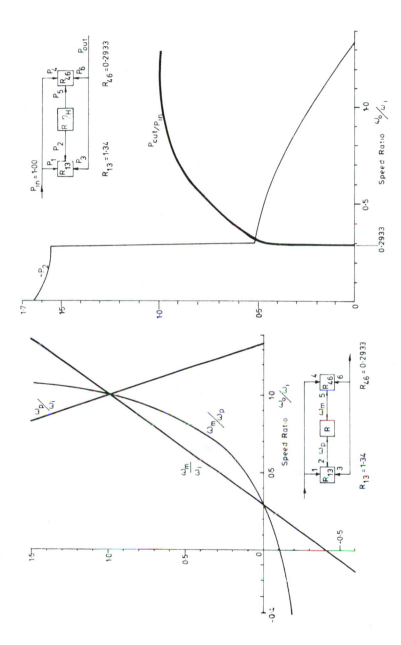

FIGURE 12.9   Double differential shunt transmission

Bibliography

1. White, R.G.S. "An experimental survey of vehicle aerodynamic characteristics" A series of reports. Motor Industry Research Association. Confidential.
2. Taborek, J.J. 1957. "Resistance Forces". 8 August p. 101. "Machine Design". Also May 30, July 15, Sept. 19, Oct. 17 and Dec. 26 1957.
3. Halling, J. and Brothers, R.G. 1964 "Automotive Design Engineering". 2 Dec. p. 69. Mechanics of the rolling wheel.
4. Hoerner, S.F. 1958. "Fluid-Dynamic Drag" published by, and for sale only by mail order directly from the author, S.F. Hoerner at 148, Busteed Drive, Midland Park, New Jersey.
5. Herts, P.B. and Ukrainetz. "Auto. — Aerodynamic drag — force analysis". Exptl. Mechs. March 67. Vol. 7 No. 3 p. 19A-22A.
6. Tenniswood, D.M. and Graetzel, H.A. 1967. "Minimum road load for electric cars". S.A.E. paper No. 670177. Automot. Eng. Congr. Jan. 9-13, 1967. 11p.
7. Slibar, A. and Desoyer, K. 1966. "Equations of motion and equivalent models of the motor vehicle and their relation to drum test results". A.T.Z. Jan. 1966 Vol. 68. No. 1 p. 13-20. M.I.R.A. trans. 33/66 25p.
8. Lanin, V.I. 1965. "Displacement of the radial reaction during the rolling of a wheel having an elastic tyre". Avtom. Prom. June 1965 No. 6 p. 30-32 (in Russian).
9. Pogosbekov, M.I. 1964. "Raising the accuracy of the theory for determining vehicle-driving-wheel speed loss". Avtom. Prom. Nov. 1964. No. 11 p. 29-30. MIRA trans. No. 36/65. 8p.
10. Savkoor, A.B. 1965. "On the friction of rubber" Wear May/June 65. Vol. 8. No. 3 p. 222-237.
11. Dawley, M.W. 1965. "Aerodynamic effects on automotive components". SAE paper No. 948A. Internat. Automot. Engng. Congr. Jan 11-15. 1965. 10p.
12. Cox, J.H. 1965. "The fleeting tire footprint" SAE paper Internat. Automot. Engng. Congr. Jan 11-15. 1965. 8p.
13. Cornish, J.J. 1965. "Some considerations of automobile lift and drag". SAE paper No. 9488. Internat. Automot. Engng. Congr. Jan 11-15, 1965. 6p.
14. Seki, K. Sasaki, S. and Tsunoda, H. 1969. "Tyre rolling resistance". Automobile Engineer. March, 1969.
15. Curtiss, W.W. 1969. "Low power loss tire". SAE paper No. 690108. Automot. Engng. Congress. Jan 13-17, 1969.
16. Anon, 1966. "A new dynamometer trailer for testing high speed cars". MIRA Bulletin No. 5. 1966.
17. Gengenbach, W. and Weber, R. 1969. "Measurement of the deflection of cross-ply and radial-ply tyres". ATZ June 1969. Vol. 71. No. 6 pp. 196-198.

18. Warholic, T.C. "Rolling Resistance Performance of passenger tires during warm-up. Speed, load and inflation pressure effects SAE p. 820455.

19. Kieselback, R. "The history of car aerodynamics". Auto, Mot Sport 22 Sept, 1982.

20. Montgomerie, G. "Economy: The answer is blowing in the wind" Comm. Mot. 8 Jan. 1983.

21. Muto, S. "The aerodynamic drag coefficient of a passenger car and methods for reducing it". Japan Auto. Res. Inst.

22. Scibor-Rylaski, A.J. "Road Vehicle Aerodynamics". Pentech Press, 1975.

23. Burkart, H. "A contribution to Rolling Resistance Measurement with Particular Emphasis in Peripheral Conditions" Automobil-Industrie. No. 3 1983.

24. Anon. "Don't throw petrol to the wind — windtunnel tests of cars and accessories" Quattroroute.

25. Hufner, H. "Calculation of drag coefficient" KFT July 1979.

26. Pershing B. et al, "Estimation of vehicle aerodynamic drag" US EPA Rep. No. EPA-460/3-76-025.

27. White, R.G.S. "A rating method for assessing vehicle aerodynamic drag coefficients" M.I.R.A. Report No. 1967/9, 1967. Confidential.

28. Doberenz, M.E. "A parametric investigation of the validity of 1/25 scale automobile aerodynamic testing" SAE p. 760189, 1976.

29. Anon. 1967. "Automotive Design Engineering". January issue, p. 44. Tyre Rolling resistance.

30. Lucas, G.G. "Vehicle Performance Calculations". Ph.D. Thesis Loughborough 1970.

31. Bevilacqua, R.M. and Percarpio, E.P. 1968. "Friction of rubber on wet surfaces". Science, Vol. 160. No. 3831 pp. 959-964. May 31 1968.

32. Bogan, R.F. and Dobbie, W.J. "Lower power use and operating temperatures give 2-ply tire the edge". SAE Journal Vol. 75 No. 10 pp. 78-81. Oct. 1967.

33. Little, L.F. 1964-5. Earth-Moving Machinery Symposium proceedings. I. Mech. E. Vol. 179 Pt. 3F. Paper 4 "Mechanics of Earth-Moving Vehicles".

34. Bekker, K.G. Off-the-road locomotion. University of Michigan Press, Ann Arbur, Michigan.

35. Reece, A.R. 1964. J. Inst. Br. Agric. Engrs. Vol. 20 (No. 2) "Theory and practice of off-the-road locomotion".

36. Payne, P.C.J., Tanner, D.W. and Spoor, G. 1964-5. Earth-moving machinery symposium proceedings. I. Mech. Engrs. Vol. 179 Pt. 3F paper 1 "A review of the relevance of soil mechanics in earth-moving".

37. Firth, B.W. 1967. "Resistance of soils to sinkage and translation of rigid bodies. A study by means of Dimensional Analysis". S.A.E. paper No. 670172. Automot. Engng. Congr. Jan. 9-13, 1967, 17p.

38. Cleare, G.V. 1963. "Factors affecting the performance of high speed track layers". I. Mech. E. Auto. Div. Advance copy ADP2/64 Dec. 10. 1963. 16p.

39. Reece, A.R. 1966. "Principles of soil-vehicle mechanics". Proc. I. Mech. E. Vol. 180. Part 2A 1965-6.

40. White, R.G.S. and Carr, G.W. 1967. "Instrumentation and Test Techniques for Motor Vehicles". I. Mech. E. Proceedings of a symposium held jointly with the

Advanced School of Automobile Engineering, Cranfield. Paper 8 entitled "Aerodynamic testing of vehicles at M.I.R.A.".

41. Easingwood-Wilson, D. et al "An instrumented car to analyse energy consumption on the road". TRRL report 787, 1977.

42. Sturm, J.M. 1962. "Acceleration and fuel measurements — New tools and techniques". S.A.E. preprint No. 471G. Automot. Engng. Congress. Jan. 8-12 1962. 8p.

43. Ardoino, G.L., Pinolini, F. and Zandona, L. "Electronic equipment for measuring motor vehicle performances on the road". Proc. I. Mech. E. Vol. 182. Part 3B pp. 130-139.

44. Fletcher, W. 1963. "The application of telemetry to the testing of motor vehicles". Proc. I. Mech. E. Vol. 178. Part 2A No. 3.

45. Lucas, G.G. "Drag data from deceleration tests" Symposium on Road Vehicle Aerodynamics sponsored by N.P.L., M.I.R.A. and R.Ae.S. held at City University London, 1969.

46. Emtage, A.L. "The vehicle coast-down test" M. Phil Thesis. Loughborough, 1983.

47. Ivens, J. and Lawser, J.J. "Experimental track test methods of estimating vehicle tractive resistance" 20th FISITA Congress, Vienna, paper No. 845105, 1984.

48. Greene, A.B. and Lucas, G.G. 1969, "The Testing of Internal Combustion Engines" English Univ. Press.

49. British Standard Code. BS5514 Part 1. Reciprocating I.C. Engines: Performance. 1982.

50. ISO 3046/1 Reciprocating I.C. Engines — Performance — Part 1: Standard reference conditions and declarations of power, fuel consumption and lubricating oil consumption.

51. I. Mech. E. Proceedings of the Drive-line 70 Conference, Jersey, 1970.

52. I. Mech. E. Proceedings of the Drive-Line 84 Conference, Auto. Division. 1984.

53. Down, D. "The passenger car power plant: Future perspectives" 19th FISITA Congress paper No. 82010 Melbourne 1982.

54. Lucas, G.G. "The motor car in the year 2000". S.E.R.C. & I. Mech. E. Proc. I. Mech. E. 198D 3 1983, London.

55. Lucas, G.G. & Mizon, R. "A model of clutch engagement" Proc. I. Mech. E. "Noise & Vibration of engines & Transmissions" Conf. Cranfield, July, 1979. See also Mizon, R. Ph.D. Thesis. Loughborough. 1974.

56. Zoeppritz, H.P. "An overview of European measuring methods and techniques". Transpn. Res. Record 621, May 1977.

57. McKenzie, R.D., Howell, W.M. and Skaar, D.E. 1967. "Computerised evaluation of drive — vehicle — terrain system". S.A.E. paper No. 670168. Automot. Engng. Congress. Jan. 9-13. 1967 13p.

58. Fourquet, M. 1965. "Calculation of car performance on electronic computers" Ingenieurs de l'Auto. Feb. 65. Vol. 36, No. 2 p. 87-93. M.I.R.A. trans. No. 53/65. 16p.

59. Ordorica, M.A. 1965. "Vehicle performance prediction" S.A.E. paper No. 650623. Detroit Section Meeting, May 10, 1965. 10p.

60. Fiala, K. 1962. "An approximate expression for the acceleration performance of

road vehicles". A.T.Z. June, 1962. Vol. 64. No 6. p. 195-196. M.I.R.A. trans. 44/62. 4p.

61. Noon, W.D. 1962. "Computer simulated vehicle performance" S.A.E. special publication No. SP240. Dec. 62 p. 22-28.

62. Setz, H.L. 1960. "Computer predicts car acceleration". SAE preprint No. 1968. Summer meeting. June 5-10, 1960. 33pp.

63. Louden, R.K. and Lukey, I. 1960. "Computer simulation of Automotive fuel economy and acceleration". SAE preprint No. 196A Summer meeting. June 5-10, 1960. 21pp.

64. Ogorkiewicz, R.M. 1960. "American Military Vehicles: Performance calculations and developments". Engineer. Dec. 23, 1960. Vol. 210. No. 5474. pp. 1054-1056.

65. Arno, R.D. and Bischoff, T.J. 1961. "Digital computer utilization in the design of the experimental truck, 2 1/2 ton XM521 at Detroit Arsenal". SAE paper 746, SAE International Congress and Exposition of Automotive Engineering. Detroit Jan 9-13, 1961.

66. Mencik, Z. et al "Simulation of wide open throttle vehicle performance" SAEp 780289. 1978.

67. Dinkel, J. "Computerized Road Testing". Road and Track, May, 1977.

68. Ordorica, M.A. 1966, "Computer idealizes vehicle design through performance study". SAE Journal, Jan. 66 Vol. 74. No. 1 p. 101-104.

69. Lavi, A. and Vogl, T.P. (Editors) 1965 "Recent Advances in Optimization Techniques", John Wiley & Sons.

70. Wilde, D.J. 1964 "Optimum seeking Methods", Prentice-Hall, Inc. Englewood Cliffs, N.J.

71. Davidon, W.C. 1959. "Variable Metric Method for Minimization" Argonne Natl. Lab. NL-5990 REv., Univ. of Chicago. 21pp.

72. Booth, A.D. 1957. "Numerical Methods", Butterworths, London.

73. Storey, C. 1962. "Application of a Hill-climbing Method of Optimization". Chem. Engrg. Sci XVIII 45-52.

74. Rosenbrock, H.H. 1960. "An Automatic method for finding the greatest or least value of a Function". The Computer J.3, 175-182.

75. Powell, M.J.D. 1964. "An efficient method for finding the minimum of a function of several variables without calculating derivatives". The Computer J. 7, 155-162.

76. Gill, P.E. and Murray, W. "Minimization subject to bounds on the variables" N.P.L. report NAC72, 1976.

77. Lucas, G.G. Stocker, R. and Mizon, R. "Correction for the effects of ambient conditions on vehicle time-to-speed results" 2nd International Conf. on Vehicle Mechanics, Paris, Sept. 1971.

78. Cornell, J.J. 1965. "Passenger car fuel economy characteristics on modern super highways" SAE Meeting Nov. 2-4, 1965. 6p.

79. Warren, G.B. 1965. "Some factors influencing motorcar fuel consumption in service". A.S.M.E. paper No. 65 — WA/APC-1. Winter Annual Meeting, No. 7-11, 1965. 6p.

80. Scheffler, C.A. and Niepoth, G.W. 1965. "Customer fuel economy estimated from engineering tests'. SAE paper No. 650862. Nat. Fuels and Lubricants

Meeting. Nov. 2-4 1965. 16p.

81. Szirtes, T. 1968. "An index to characterise the overall fuel economy of an internal combustion engine". A.S.M.E. paper 68-WA/DGP-2. Winter annual meeting Dec. 1-5, 1968.

82. Kronogara, S.O. and Rosen, C.G.A. 1969. "Matching gas turbine propulsion systems to vehicles". SAE paper No. 680539, West coast meeting, San Francisco. Aug. 12-15.

83. Smith, F.B., Meyer, W.A.O. and Ayres, R.W. 1969. "A statistical approach to describing vehicular driving cycles". SAE paper. No. 690212. Automotive Engineering Congress Jan. 13-17.

84. Genbom, V.V., Nitikin, N.N and Khoma, S.S. 1969. "A method for the complex investigation of the influence of engine and transmission parameters on the tractive and speed characteristics and fuel economy of vehicles". Avtom. Prom. No. 2 p. 5-8. Feb. 1969.

85. Hwang, D.N. 1968. "Fundamental parameters of vehicle fuel economy and acceleration". SAE paper No. 690541. Detroit Section October 30, 1968.

86. OECD "Automobile fuel consumption in actual traffic conditions" OECD. Dec, 1981.

87. Weeks, R. "Fuel consumption of a diesel and a petrol car" Transport and Road Research Lab. report TRRL 964, 1982.

88. Kuhlmann, P. "Studies of fuel consumption in urban driving" ATZ, Jan, 1982. p. 299.

89. Renouf, M.A. "An analysis of the fuel consumption of commercial vehicles by computer simulation". TRRL report No. 973, 1981.

90. Knoros, V.I. 1968. "The influence of tyre rolling resistance on vehicle fuel consumption". Avtom. Prom. March. 68. No. 3. p. 11-14 (in Russian).

91. Bland, P.G. 1966. "Saving weight means saving money". Bus and Coach. Vol. 38 No. 1. Jan. 1966. p. 2-6.

92. Muller, A.T. 1966. "The performance of commercial vehicles with different power plants" Eleventh F.I.S.I.T.A. congress. Preprint No. A.6. June 12-16, 1966. 29p M.I.R.A. trans. 66/66 32p.

93. Annand, W.J.D. 1965. "Power for commercial vehicles — A comparison of claims". Eng. Des. and Appl. June, 65. Vol. 1 No. 9 p. 4-9.

94. Joyner, J.A. 1965. "Factors affecting fuel economy in diesel powered vehicles". SAE paper No. 650430. Mid-year meeting, Chicago. May 17-21. 1965. 11p.

95. Cato, W.G. and Meek, J.F. 1961. "Improvement of fuel economy by minor changes in aerodynamic shape". SAE special publication. S.P. 195. April, 1961. pp. 4-7.

96. Minervini, T. 1968. "Effect of Aerodynamic drag on the cost of transport by motorway". A.T.A. Dec. 1968. Vol. 21 No. 12. pp. 664-666. MIRA trans. 14/69.

97. Molly, R. 1966. "Hydrostatic vehicle transmission — Their arrangement and design". A.T.Z. Oct. 1966. Vol. 68. No. 10 p. 339-346. MIRA trans. No. 56/67.

98. Worn, C.L.G. and Walker, A.C. 1965. "A gearbox replacement hydrostatic drive". SAE paper No. 650689. Farm Construction and Industrial Machinery meeting. Sept. 13-16, 1965. 12p.

99. Everall, P.F. 1968. "The affect of road and traffic conditions on fuel consumption". RRL Report No. Lr 226.

100. Webb, C.R. 1952. "The effect of gradient on fuel consumption and speed of a road vehicle". Proc. I. Mech. E. (Auto. Div.) 1952-3.

101. Frohlick H. et al. "Fuel consumption reduction through drivetrain optimisation in commercial vehicles". KFT May 1983.

102. Janssen, L.R. et al. "Aerodynamic improvements — A great potential for better fuel economy" SAEp 780265, 1978.

103. Frode, W. 1966. "Recent Developments in the NSU Wankel engine". James Clayton Lecture. Proc. I. Mech. E. A.D Vol. 180 Part 2A. Advance copy ADL 2/66.

104. Anon. 1968. "Leyland Gas Turbine Tractor". Automobile Engineer. Dec. 1968.

105. Giles, J.G. 1966. "Variable ratio transmissions and vehicle operating economy". Mobile Research Symposium paper May 3-4 1966. 12p.

106. Martin, G. "Choosing gearbox ratios for on-road vehicles" Automot. Engr. Oct/ Nov. 1981.

107. Giles, J.G. 1961. "Automatic and Fluid Transmissions" Odhams Press Ltd.

108. Reinke "Torque converter and hydrostatic transmissions — History and Comparison" SAEp 821105, 1982.

109. Lucas, G.G. and Rayner, A. 1968. "Torque converter design calculations". Automobile Engineer Vol. 60 No. 2 Feb. 1970.

110. Forster, H.J. 1963, "Torque Conversion range and gear ratios in automotive transmissions'. Automobile Industrie Dec. 63. p. 107-130 M.I.R.A. trans. No. 49/65. 71p.

111. Wilson, W.E. and Lemme, C.D. 1968. "The hydro-mechanical transmission — Ideal and Real". SAE paper No. 680605 Combined meeting Sept. 9-12, 1968.

112. Lucas, G.G. "Calculation of torque converter performance on over-run, in reverse and when the reaction member is driven from the output shaft" Automotive Engineer, Vol. 12, No. 4, 1977.

113. Lucas, G.G., Cropley, C. and Hobbs, H. "Design and Performance of the Ratcliffe/Hobbs Continually Variable Automatic Transmission Proc. I. Mech. E. paper C356/80 of "Systems Engineering in Land Transport". London, Sept, 1980.

114. Ott, A. June 1966. "Calculations of Driving Performance with reference to torque converter and power changing" Preprint No. A.10. Eleventh F.I.S.I.T.A. congress M.I.R.A. translation No. 9/67 by R.J.H. Milne.

115. Lucas, G.G. "A Technique for calculating the time to speed of an automatic transmission vehicle". Proc. I. Mech. E. Drive-line 70, Jersey, April, 1970.

116. Forster, H.J. 1966. "The effect of Automatic Transmissions on Performance and Fuel Consumption". Part I. A.T.Z. Oct. 1966. Vol. 68. No. 10. pp. 337-339. M.I.R.A. translation 53/67. 22p.

117. Forster, H.J. 1965. "The influence of Automatic transmissions on road performance and fuel consumption". The Chartered Mechanical Engineer Nov. 1965. pp. 611-615.

118. White, G. "Properties of differential transmissions". The Engineer, July 1967.

119. Lucas, G.G. "Expressions Governing the power flow through differential

mechanisms having imperfect efficiencies". Proc. I. Mech. E. Auto. Div. C12/84 Drive-Line 84.

120. Fellows, T.G., Dowson, D., Perry, G. and Plint, M.A. "Perbury continuously variable ratio transmission" Proc. of Symposium on Auto. Transmissions "Advances in Automobile Engrg. Part II" Pergamon Press 1964.

121. Callaghan, J.M. "Belt Drive Transmission Gears up for the 80's" Automot. Inds. 1980.

122. MacMillan, R.H. 1964. "The control of stepless variable speed transmissions in automobiles and their possible application to regenerative systems". Tenth FISITA congress. Tokyo, May, 1964.

123. MacMillan, R.H. and Davies, P.B. 1965. "Analytical study of systems for bifurcated power transmissions". Journal Mech. Engrg. Sci. Vol. 7. No. 1. 1965 pp. 40-47.

124. White, G. and Christie, D.M. 1967. "Improving the speed-holding ability of a variable — ratio transmission by means of differential coupling". Int. J. Mach Tool Des. Res. Vol. 7, pp. 155-168. Pergamon Press.

125. Ross, W.A. "Designing a hydromechanical transmission for heavy trucks" SAEp 720725. 1972.

126. Stubbs, P.W.R. "Development of a Perbury traction transmission for motor car applications" ASME paper No. 80-C2/DET-59 1980.

Index

199